CW00736277

Praise

'In *At Home in Lent* Gordon Giles has elevated the everyday to the realm of spiritual reflection and meditation in a way which is both simple and profound. Gordon's reflections are helpfully reminiscent of expressions of Celtic spirituality, where we find prayers for the cooking pot and for lighting a fire. A most accessible guide and accompaniment with which to navigate Lent, with just the right amount of challenge and affirmation, particularly for those leading busy lives. As Gordon has bravely used the toilet as an area for reflection, it is safe to say that this book might well be used in the smallest room as well as on the train or in a prayer space.'

Revd Prebendary Dr Neil Evans, canon steward of St Paul's Cathedral

Praise for At Home in Advent

'This book invites us to take Advent and the Christmas season seriously. By using a number of meditations based on commonplace articles like traffic lights, burglar alarms and even Christmas jumpers, Gordon Giles unlocks the meanings of the story that shapes the time of year. The book has a definite context, having been written during the tight lockdown of early 2020, which makes it even more relevant. We have all become far more acquainted with our own houses, and a book that seeks to see the spiritual significance of this is therefore most valuable. The author tackles issues of expectation, waiting, mortality and hope as well as celebrating the joy of the incarnation and the salvation that Jesus brought. This is a first-class read and a valuable aid for the Advent and Christmas seasons.'

Cavan Wood, *Transforming Ministry*

15 The Chambers, Vineyard
Abingdon OX14 3FE
brf.org.uk

Bible Reading Fellowship (BRF) is a charity (233280)
and company limited by guarantee (301324),
registered in England and Wales

ISBN 978 1 80039 115 4
First published 2023
10 9 8 7 6 5 4 3 2 1 0
All rights reserved

Acknowledgements

Unless otherwise stated, scripture quotations are taken from The New
Revised Standard Version of the Bible, Anglicised edition, copyright © 1989,
1995 by the Division of Christian Education of the National Council of the
Churches of Christ in the United States of America. Used by permission.
All rights reserved.

A catalogue record for this book is available from the British Library

Printed and bound by CPI Group (UK) Ltd, Croydon CR0 4YY

AT HOME

and Out & About

52 biblical contemplations
on faith, hope and love
for a re-emerging world

Gordon Giles

This book is, to some extent, a farewell and thank-you gift to the people of St Mary Magdalene's, Enfield, whom I had to leave without ceremony during lockdown in 2020 after 17 years as their vicar. To them my family and I owe a huge debt of gratitude for faith, hope and love.

I would also like to thank friends and colleagues Stephen, Olivia, Dan, Jonathan, Phil, Matthew, Chris, Sue, Belinda and all at Rochester Cathedral and elsewhere who, whether they realised it or not, have contributed to the creation of this book. And to Jessica and Maria, as always.

Contents

AUTUMN

ADVENT

CHRISTMAS

NEW YEAR

WINTER

LENT

PASSIONTIDE

EASTER

Introduction

In 2020 and 2021 we were at home in Advent and at home in Lent. These were difficult, fearful, even tearful times, on which we look back with sorrow and upon which we continue to reflect. We shall never forget a year or more of lockdowns and the impact they had on our living and loving, our freedoms, wishes and relationships. And for so many the sense of closure when a loved one died has been hard, if not impossible, to achieve.

Yet amid the clouds of poison vapour that the coronavirus spread over the globe, there were also signs of hope, acts of human kindness and sparks of divine light flickering in the penitential and solemn glooms of the seasons of Advent and Lent. Christmas 2020 struggled to be a season of light, and the baubles were very hollow indeed as Christmas dinners and parties were cancelled or prohibited, and families denied what, for many, 'Christmas is all about': family, fellowship, eating, drinking and making merry. It was a deprivation for all, necessitated by a deadly and real fear of something beyond our control and to which, through government intervention, we had no choice but to submit. The coronavirus had real power over us, and to some extent, still does. The same cloud hung over Christmas 2021. It was not until Easter 2022 that many felt any sense of normality resuming.

The virus controlled us in two ways. It restricted our freedom to do as we pleased and to meet whomsoever we wanted and roam wherever we wanted. It exercised a physical and practical dominion, the extent and range of which hardly needs describing. Covid-19 exercised a spiritual dominion too. For it closed our churches, deprived us of singing hymns and carols and forced us to wear masks when we were finally allowed back in. More significantly, it changed the spiritual landscape of faith, and *made* us think, act and pray differently. Initially this was thought of by many as a destructive power, while others embraced the new opportunities for praise, worship and service, and it became a creative power. Good may yet come from this, if it has not already.

Even though this book was written during the major period of coronavirus restrictions and emergence, it is not my purpose to retell the story or rehearse the drama of the coronavirus in the UK and elsewhere. It is a story we all know well, and we have our own parts in it, some labouring tirelessly backstage, others in the limelight. Many of us were simply in the audience, powerless but emotionally engaged in the tragedy unfolding before and around us. We have been at home in Lent and Advent, and perhaps you even read the two books I wrote whose titles and content serendipitously summed up our state of being in 2020 and 2021 – *At Home in Lent* and *At Home in Advent*. But now it is time to go out and about with God, to reclaim and renew our spiritual engagement with God's world in which we dwell and move and have our being. God has not changed. The world has not changed. Jesus Christ has not changed. But we have. This is not a problem, but an opportunity.

So I invite you to leave Lent and Advent at home on the shelf, and come and explore the world in the wake of Covid-19 – to reflect on what has changed and to re-engage with what has not. The Covid pandemic has to some extent given way to other phenomena to engage with and reflect upon: the attack on Ukraine, energy and cost-of-living crises, environmental concerns and the death of Queen Elizabeth II. These events bring challenges and traumas, emotional upheaval and real cause for worry. There is always something to worry about, something to pray about, something to reflect on. Yet we must not lose sight of Covid-19, for it affected us in ways that nothing we can remember ever has.

This is not a Lent book nor an Advent book, although it may be read in any season. It can be read from Eastertide to Eastertide weekly, and is laid out with that in mind, but its 52 chapters can be read week by week at any point of the year, or on consecutive days, or even randomly. As with *At Home in Lent* and its successor *At Home in Advent*, the theme of each chapter is an object, activity or phenomenon about which we might learn and on which we might reflect under God. As we re-emerge into a world that is both scarred and healed of the corona-virus to varying degrees, we encounter the familiar in new ways and the unfamiliar in old ways. We are changed and it is time to embrace that, for we cannot resist or deny it.

Voltaire's atheistic hero Candide concluded that we live in 'the best of all possible worlds'. The apostle Paul wrote that 'we know that all things work together for good for those who love God, who are called according to his purpose' (Romans 8:28). And Jesus, in our joys and sorrows, calls us over the tumults of the world to follow him, love him and to find faith, hope and love in all things. For God has a good purpose in all the hard things that happen to his people and, in Christ the good shepherd, provides a gateway to eternal, abundant life (John 10:10).

So let us walk on, to roam from home and go out and about in God's world of hope and promise.

Easter

1 Social distancing

Mary stood weeping outside the tomb. As she wept, she bent over to look into the tomb; and she saw two angels in white, sitting where the body of Jesus had been lying, one at the head and the other at the feet. They said to her, 'Woman, why are you weeping?' She said to them, 'They have taken away my Lord, and I do not know where they have laid him.' When she had said this, she turned around and saw Jesus standing there, but she did not know that it was Jesus. Jesus said to her, 'Woman, why are you weeping? For whom are you looking?' Supposing him to be the gardener, she said to him, 'Sir, if you have carried him away, tell me where you have laid him, and I will take him away.' Jesus said to her, 'Mary!' She turned and said to him in Hebrew, 'Rabbouni!' (which means Teacher). Jesus said to her, 'Do not hold on to me, because I have not yet ascended to the Father. But go to my brothers and say to them, "I am ascending to my Father and your Father, to my God and your God."' Mary Magdalene went and announced to the disciples, 'I have seen the Lord'; and she told them that he had said these things to her…

A week later his disciples were again in the house, and Thomas was with them. Although the doors were shut, Jesus came and stood among them and said, 'Peace be with you.' Then he said to Thomas, 'Put your finger here and see my hands. Reach out your hand and put it in my side. Do not doubt but believe.' Thomas answered him, 'My Lord and my God!'

JOHN 20:11–18, 26–28

We are Easter people, and 'Alleluia' is our song. Yet in Easter 2020 churches were closed and clergy told to stay away to slow down the Covid-19 infection rate. For the first time in living memory, we were told that how we behaved had a real impact on the life and death of others.

We have to look a long way back into history for parallels. In 1208, King John refused to accept Pope Innocent's archbishop of Canterbury, Stephen Langton. So the pope put England under an 'interdict' which endured between March 1208 and July 1214, and clergy could not celebrate the sacraments. In 1348 the Black Death killed half the population of England. The Great Plague of 1665–66 killed an estimated 100,000 people, almost a quarter of London's population, in 18 months. The next bubonic plague pandemic, known as the 'Third Pandemic', lasted from 1855 to as recently as 1960, emerging at various places in the world throughout that period.

There are various aspects of modern lockdowns which can be traced back to pandemics of long ago. A novel one this time, however, was 'social distancing'. Whether it was two metres, or 'one metre plus' (involving mask wearing), we were told to stay away from other people. Pews were cordoned off and chairs were repositioned in churches (the vergers at Rochester Cathedral had a special two-metre stick they used) and signs appeared in supermarkets and streets alike, exhorting us to 'Keep your distance'. We still see some of those signs, or footprints on the ground, which will remind us for years to come.

Jesus' words to Mary Magdalene when she encountered him at the garden tomb resonate with the newfound phenomenon of social distancing. 'Do not hold on to me,' he says, or, as the Latin Vulgate puts it, '*Noli me tangere*' – 'Do not touch me.' These are harrowing words for Mary to hear, whose natural reaction is to want to embrace her Lord amid the delightful confusion of realising he is alive.

Artists who have depicted this famous scene – Fra Angelico, Titian and Holbein among them – have presented an emotional snapshot of this beautiful, terrifying, alienating moment. Mary reaches out to Jesus, who leans away in a gesture of what we might paradoxically think of as loving rejection. For in these images there is separation, a breaking loose of the human in God, as Jesus reveals that he will ascend and, in bodily form, be gone. She cannot touch him and nor can we. So close, yet so far. The joy of the encounter is shot through with the wrenching pain of separation.

Those who visited elderly relatives in care homes or friends, those whom we embrace or even greet with a warm handshake, know something of this agony as we were told, not by God but the state, 'Do not touch.' It is better for everyone if you do not, we were told; it will only cause further pain; it is dangerous; you will do more harm than good; it is selfish, and satisfies your needs but does not serve others; do not administer the kiss of death inadvertently. Some people are more 'touchy-feely' than others, for sure, so social distancing caused varying degrees of angst. Yet for many the lack of touch from others, particularly for those who live alone, was agonising and adherence to social distancing rules became sacrificial. Meanwhile others did not conform, sometimes with dire consequences. Every death from Covid-19 was a tragedy of its own, but none more so than those which resulted from deliberate ignorance, rejection or resistance to medical advice to not come into close contact with or touch those whom we love. It was not only about not becoming infected, but also about not infecting others.

Social distancing, while being a form of mini-quarantine, based on the scientific study of the distribution of aerosol particles in breath, was nevertheless one of the toughest dimensions of Covid-19 precautions. When in summer 2021, the prime minister said it was okay to hug someone again, the relief was palpable. The return to shaking hands and hugging seemed strange after not doing so. Yet at least it meant that the long Lent of social distancing was over and the ability to renew human touch was resurrected.

When Jesus first appeared to the disciples in the upper room, he showed them the marks of passion which proved his resurrection. But like Mary in the garden, they did not touch him. Thomas was absent and did not believe. So when Jesus returned, he invited Thomas to touch him. The time was right. It is important to be able to touch and hold others; their bodily presence is as important as emotional and spiritual presence. In the faith, hope and love the risen Christ gives us, we have all three: spiritual faith, emotional hope and loving touch. These three abide, and they abide, as the risen Christ himself does, in us, with us and through us.

The ability to touch others was denied and then restored. This was a kind of death and resurrection of its own, and Mary felt it keenly in the garden. Yet the resurrection is truly good news for all of us, at home or out and about, inside or out, now and always. For the risen Christ is with us always, to the end of the age (Matthew 28:20). Thus we *are* Easter people, and 'Alleluia' *is* our song.

Give us your Easter joy, O Jesus, and even if distanced from others, draw us close to you, that we may embrace a world blossoming with resurrection hope, faith and love. Amen

Spring

2 Flowers

My beloved speaks and says to me:
'Arise, my love, my fair one,
   and come away;
for now the winter is past,
   the rain is over and gone.
The flowers appear on the earth;
   the time of singing has come,
and the voice of the turtle-dove
   is heard in our land.
The fig tree puts forth its figs,
   and the vines are in blossom;
   they give forth fragrance.
Arise, my love, my fair one,
   and come away...
Catch us the foxes,
   the little foxes,
that ruin the vineyards –
   for our vineyards are in blossom.'

My beloved is mine and I am his;
   he pastures his flock among the lilies.

SONG OF SONGS 2:10–13, 15–16

Spring is flower time, and the range of blossoms and blooms is a joy to behold. The colours and fragrances and the sheer diversity of the sequence of them lifts the spirits, even in the deepest gloom of sorrow, grief or loss. Flowers are given or used in so many contexts, but generally flowers cheer us up.

The seasons of the year and the seasons of life are punctuated and painted with petals. Christmas poinsettias; February snowdrops, crocuses, and Valentine's Day roses; March daffodils; April tulips, magnolias and cherry blossoms, and Easter lilies; May bluebells and orchids; June honeysuckles and freesias; July periwinkles and lilacs; August cornflowers and dahlias; September sunflowers and irises; October delphiniums and phlox; November carnations and winter jasmine.

Baptisms, weddings and funerals attract flowers, given for decoration, sympathy, love and friendship. Flowers adorn churches seasonally and symbolically, often for thanksgiving, remembrance or seasonal flavour. Poinsettias represent the Christmas star and lilies at Easter represent resurrection hope.

In Derbyshire from April to July, the tradition of 'well-dressing' has grown up over centuries. People collect petals from seasonal flowers and create a scene, invariably biblical, which is placed near the village well. The pagan origins may be obscure and the well no longer in use, but the artistic tradition has persisted and thrived. The well which raises water to nourish plant and animal life is annually decorated in thanksgiving with the very petals it has nourished. It is an artificial object created from, and in celebration of, natural ingredients, with the well being blessed and thanksgiving offered to God for community life, rejuvenating rain and renewing sunlight.

Flowers are reproductive phenomena, attracting insects for pollina-tion. Some flowers, such as the bee orchid, even impersonate insects to get the job done. Yet the attraction transcends purpose, providing what as humans we may consider to be unnecessary beauty. Flowers do not *need* to appeal to *us*, and so we appreciate them for no reason other than pure ocular and nasal delight. We receive this as a natural, divine gift. We rejoice in the colour, scent and beauty of nature and give God the thanks, whether in the wild, garden, church or home.

Jesus uses flowers as an illustration to exhort us to not worry about clothing, food or drink, or anything: 'Consider the lilies, how they grow: they neither toil nor spin; yet I tell you, even Solomon in all his glory was not clothed like one of these' (Luke 12:27). The reference to King Solomon resonates with the Song of Songs, which is an extended love poem, rich in euphemism and symbolism. Flowers play their metaphorical part most famously in today's passage, where alongside foxes and birds the blooming of flowers heralds spring, the reproductive season. Recall that this passage is an invitation from a man to a woman to get up (for she has swooned in love a few verses earlier) and take a romantic walk in the countryside, during which one thing might lead to another. It will not be a wanton rampage, similar to the way foxes tear up vineyards, but something sweet and lovely, like the beloved's face.

The floricultural industry struggled during the pandemic. Countries such as Kenya and the Netherlands were hard hit. It was not simply that the events which they adorned florally did not happen; workforce shortages, travel restrictions and shop closures also took their toll. Whatever we may say about the need for beauty in our lives, flowers were not an essential product in lockdowns.

Yet flowers *are* essential: their purpose in nature as part of a global ecosystem that replicates and reproduces, ultimately bearing fruit for all creation, is vital. Their metaphorical meaning is a cause of delight and reflection too, for they have a gospel message for us.

Flowers, like stars, speak of the extravagant, creative, renewing power of God. They stand fragile in the field, with their faces turned to the heavens from which pour down rays of renewing light and warmth. We all need the light of God's loving presence to illuminate dark days of fear, isolation and sorrow. We all need the warmth of God's loving touch, ministered through and to each other in human embrace. Solomon's love lyric combines flowers and human love in an embrace that transcends the words employed. The absence of flowers in our land during the lockdown seasons parallels the absence of love, and it is that which we missed being able to see, hold, smell and touch.

The return of fresh flowers to our gardens, shops and vases gives us fresh hope that restrictions can be, if not escaped, managed season-ally. The return of flowers reminds us that 'all shall be well and all manner of thing shall be well', as Julian of Norwich put it. Or as Jesus said, 'if God so clothes the grass of the field, which is alive today and tomorrow is thrown into the oven, how much more will he clothe you… Instead, strive for his kingdom, and these things will be given to you as well' (Luke 12:28, 31). This cyclical rejuvenation, in which light, warmth, renewal and hope blossom is a blooming metaphor for the Eastertide in which it flourishes.

Every flower is a resurrection, the green blade and floral cup rising from the buried bulb or seed. Our liturgical seasons mirror the seasons of the earth, and the seasons of the earth reveal themselves in an ongoing pattern of rise and fall which reminds us of the passing of time, the diurnal round, the lunar cycle and the earthly orbit. All of these add up to and are contained within the resurrection hope, brought forth on the eighth day of creation, in which faith, hope and love are revealed in the bursting of the tomb on the third, resurrection day. Every time a flower blooms, it is a mini resurrection, heralding the eternal hopefulness of creation and the everlasting promise of resurrection life. Give thanks for resurrection life revealed in every flower of the field.

Eternal God, you bless the earth with shoots, buds, flowers and fruits. As you give them life, nourish us with the rain of divine mercy, the warmth of the sun of righteousness and the light rays of your presence among us, revealed in our risen Saviour Jesus Christ. Amen

3 Family meals

> Six days before the Passover Jesus came to Bethany, the home
> of Lazarus, whom he had raised from the dead. There they
> gave a dinner for him. Martha served, and Lazarus was one
> of those at the table with him. Mary took a pound of costly
> perfume made of pure nard, anointed Jesus' feet, and wiped
> them with her hair. The house was filled with the fragrance of
> the perfume. But Judas Iscariot, one of his disciples (the one
> who was about to betray him), said, 'Why was this perfume
> not sold for three hundred denarii and the money given to the
> poor?' (He said this not because he cared about the poor, but
> because he was a thief; he kept the common purse and used
> to steal what was put into it.) Jesus said, 'Leave her alone. She
> bought it so that she might keep it for the day of my burial.
> You always have the poor with you, but you do not always
> have me.'
>
> JOHN 12:1–8

There is much eating in the Bible. This is not surprising, as all creatures need to eat. Some eat other creatures, which troubles some
people. This food chain extends from large beasts all the way down to
algae. From the fruit in the garden of Eden to the heavenly banquet,
this primary function of animal life is woven through the Bible's
journey of hope through the story of human life on earth and beyond.

Yet while every animal eats, no other animal does so at a table or in
front of the TV. Animals eat to live, while it may be said that some
people live to eat. It is certainly a pleasure for many, and not only

of taste and smell. The French philosopher Jean Anthelme Brillat-Savarin (1755–1826) wrote a treatise called 'The Philosopher in the Kitchen' (*Physiologie du Goût*), in which he said that eating is about a need being satisfied. By contrast the 'pleasures of the table' are sensations affected by the circumstances of the meal, such as the purpose of the gathering, conversation, company and fellowship. These pleasures of the table are unique to humanity, being dependent on the preparation of the meal, the venue and those present. Thus mere consumers of food become table companions. The word 'companion' means 'to eat bread with'. Food is not simply fuel: eating is a social activity.

The sociability of eating – the companionship of the table – and the communion of the eucharistic bread and wine were denied or restricted during the Covid-19 pandemic. Restaurants closed, and people were not allowed to dine with anyone except within a narrowly defined family or friendship 'bubble'. Christmas dinners in 2020 were cancelled. For many, the Christmas dinner is *the* family meal: the annual gathering which can be caricatured as a gluttonous party or piously as a 'spiritual' occasion of fellowship, generosity and goodwill made popular by Charles Dickens. What we learned in 2020 was that such meals are far more than either of these things, and we had not fully appreciated it until deprived. Christmas dinners, like birthdays, are events by which we measure our lives. In any given year there can be a new person present or someone missing from the table – someone who has been born, joined the family or who has died during the preceding year. Every year, thousands of people eat their last Christmas dinner. So in 2020 it was practically painful and poignant as many were denied a feast which, whether interpreted as being sacred or secular, is fundamentally social.

Some families do this kind of thing every week, and so were denied the 'Sunday roast' for many consecutive weeks. The tradition has waned, perhaps, but the ability to meet as a family, with grandparents, grown-up children and little ones for a family meal to share fellowship and news is both a gift and a necessity. For some in lockdown or 'shielding', the isolation was drawn out by the absence of any family 'ritual' and the loss of the normal markings of the passing of time. For others, food was left on doorsteps by neighbours, family or friends, who stepped back and waved – this was the limited companionship that some people shared, albeit vital and caring as it so often was.

It is easy to forget now that that was all that was permitted, and underneath it all was the real fear that if these rules were not observed, there might not be another family meal for some. And indeed, for some there wasn't. For we do not always have our family with us. Children grow up, leave home and make their own families. Parents and grandparents do not live forever, and we all age slowly but surely, gaining a different position and perspective on the chain of life measured out in the food we eat and with whom we eat it.

Nevertheless, meals taken together can be celebrations – even a 'wake' after a funeral. One of the ironies of funeral gatherings is that people meet relatives and friends of friends whom they have not seen for a long time. Some say with dark humour or morosity that they only meet these people at funerals. During the pandemic there seemed to be little to celebrate, while parties and large gatherings were arguably not only unsafe but also inappropriate and, at times, illegal.

The account of Jesus dining with Mary, Martha and Lazarus only days before his death has a funereal dimension to it. It was their final meal together, and no expense was spared. Although Judas questioned the cost of the perfume (which is part of the whole experience, as Brillat-Savarin might have put it), sometimes extravagance is permitted at a special gathering. Many people take this very same attitude to festivals and birthdays. The expenditure not only creates a social event of quality, but it makes it memorable: a highlight of life to be shared, relished, memorised, talked about, relived. In this sense such a meal becomes almost eucharistic: a meal of thanksgiving and remembrance. Through all the changing scenes of life, we remain in table fellowship with our companion Lord Jesus, who not only dined with his wider family at Bethany, but dines with us still, offering himself in bread and wine, that we may always be part of his family, may remember his final meal, talk about it and relive it as a recurring highlight of our ongoing lives. Every family meal is a parable of this and a foretaste of heavenly reunion.

Lord Jesus, who gave yourself as spiritual food and sustains us through joy and sorrow, be present in all our eating, that whether we dine alone or with friends and family, there is always a place for you in our hearts until that day when we shall feast together in your eternal kingdom. Amen

4 Hospitality

Two of them were going to a village called Emmaus, about seven miles from Jerusalem... While they were talking and discussing, Jesus himself came near and went with them, but their eyes were kept from recognising him...

As they came near the village to which they were going, he walked ahead as if he were going on. But they urged him strongly, saying, 'Stay with us, because it is almost evening and the day is now nearly over.' So he went in to stay with them. When he was at the table with them, he took bread, blessed and broke it, and gave it to them. Then their eyes were opened, and they recognised him; and he vanished from their sight. They said to each other, 'Were not our hearts burning within us while he was talking to us on the road, while he was opening the scriptures to us?'

LUKE 24:13–16, 28–32

As we saw in the previous chapter, hospitality was a major casualty of the Covid-19 pandemic. Hotels, restaurants, pubs, cafes and fast-food chains were not allowed to serve customers: only takeaways and deliveries were permitted. Broadly speaking, hospitality was banned and no one could visit anyone else to eat unless they were part of their social or family 'bubble'.

The psychological impact of this was long-lasting, and this deprivation both reminded people of how much they missed it and may also have changed habits, such that dining out and visiting others' homes has become something we only used to do. It is sociologically interesting that the British government introduced a scheme in summer 2020 whereby the population were encouraged to 'eat out to help out', subsidising up to half the cost of doing so. On one level it was an attempt to get the hospitality industry back on its feet, but on another was an underlying recognition that social dining has an impact on our well-being and is not something which should fall victim to the virus. It is also to be remembered that the intention was for *families* (in the broad sense of the word) to eat together. Nevertheless the scheme could not last and further lockdowns followed.

Hospitality is a two-way, covenantal – almost contractual – matter. This is, of course, explicitly the case in a restaurant or café, where money changes hands, customers have expectations of quality, service and hygiene, and landlords and managers have conventions of politeness and honesty to which they adhere and expect of customers. But there is also a social contract when we invite others into our homes. While some people are more hospitable than others, there is pleasure on both sides of the host–guest equation: it is a delight to welcome guests, to prepare, cook and share far more than the meal itself. Similarly, to accept an invitation to someone else's home is to assume conventions of respect, politeness, gratitude and kindness. One convention that has endured is that the gift of hospitality offered is invariably met with a gift brought by the guests: wine, flowers or chocolates, for example. I remember, many years ago, a house guest arriving with a chair as a gift, although that was because on the previous visit he had sat on a chair and it had broken under his weight!

Hospitality is an ancient tradition in many cultures and faiths, and it has strong Christian roots too, planted in the rich soil of Judaism; for example, Abraham welcoming the three 'angels' (Genesis 18) and Jesus sending out his disciples in the expectation that they will receive hospitality (Mark 6:10–12).

The story of the risen Christ meeting two disciples on the road to Emmaus is significant, not only because it is about their recognition of Jesus in the breaking of bread, but also because it is a mirror image of the hospitality God offers us in Christ. At the last supper, Jesus hosts a Passover meal, welcoming the disciples – and us – to a heavenly meal on earth, opening the doors of eternity to we who are but travellers on the road. A few days later the opportunity for humanity to return divine hospitality arises, and the unwary walking companions invite Jesus to their table, which itself is at an inn offering hospitality to all who pass by. Just as we are invited to accept the welcome offered by Jesus into the kingdom of God, he accepts their human hospitality, which resonates with his humble birth and welcoming on earth by mere shepherds; born in a feeding trough in Bethlehem (which means 'house of bread').

In fact, Luke's gospel is full of meals and feeding, which culminate in this journey to the Emmaus dinner table at which humankind invites *him* to *our* table, a kindly act on behalf of humanity which barely balances the meagre offering of praise and thanksgiving which we can offer to the host of the heavenly banquet.

The story has had a profound influence subsequently, not least on St Benedict, whose Benedictine Order place a special emphasis on hospitality: he reminded them that 'All guests who present themselves are to be welcomed as Christ, for he will say: I was a stranger and you made me welcome' (*Order of Benedict* 53:1). From hospitality offered in human kindness we get the concept of hospitals, which were not always purely medical establishments, with their heritage being traceable back through knightly orders such as the Hospitallers of St John, whose origin lies in an 11th-century hospital founded in Jerusalem by Italian merchants to care for sick and poor pilgrims. Subsequently the Order was based in Cyprus, Rhodes and then Malta, but are probably most well known in the UK for their connections to St John's Ambulance, who have been caring for strangers since being created in 1877.

This may seem a long way removed from ordering a pint at the local pub or dining with neighbours, yet at the root of all hospitality there is both theological and humanitarian giving and receiving. Even Jesus received as well as gave, and in his case, as well as any other, it is true that it is in giving that we receive. Those travellers who invited Jesus to supper received far more than they gave, and so it is when we invite guests into our homes. We not only invite the persons themselves, with their stories, wisdom, insights, conversation and friendship; we also invite them as fellow beings made in the image of God, in whom, therefore, we see the face of Jesus Christ. So often they give us far more than we give them. Those who fed Jesus on the road to Emmaus gave him bread. In return he gave them a spiritual feast served by the one who is the bread of life.

Next time you eat out, remember the hospitable landlord in Emmaus, his guests and their companion on the road, and pray for all who have no opportunity to give or receive hospitality.

Generous God, you welcome us sinners to sit and eat at your table. Help us to see your face in all those with whom we eat and drink, that we, unworthy as we are, may glimpse the kingdom to which you invite us all through Jesus Christ our Saviour. Amen

5 Baptisms

[John said]: 'I baptise you with water for repentance, but one who is more powerful than I is coming after me; I am not worthy to carry his sandals. He will baptise you with the Holy Spirit and fire. His winnowing-fork is in his hand, and he will clear his threshing-floor and will gather his wheat into the granary; but the chaff he will burn with unquenchable fire.'

Then Jesus came from Galilee to John at the Jordan, to be baptised by him. John would have prevented him, saying, 'I need to be baptised by you, and do you come to me?' But Jesus answered him, 'Let it be so now; for it is proper for us in this way to fulfil all righteousness.' Then he consented. And when Jesus had been baptised, just as he came up from the water, suddenly the heavens were opened to him and he saw the Spirit of God descending like a dove and alighting on him. And a voice from heaven said, 'This is my Son, the Beloved, with whom I am well pleased.'

Now the eleven disciples went to Galilee, to the mountain to which Jesus had directed them. When they saw him, they worshipped him; but some doubted. And Jesus came and said to them, 'All authority in heaven and on earth has been given to me. Go therefore and make disciples of all nations, baptising them in the name of the Father and of the Son and of the Holy Spirit, and teaching them to obey everything that I have commanded you. And remember, I am with you always, to the end of the age.'

MATTHEW 3:11–17; 28:16–20

While it is widely acknowledged that anyone can be baptised at any age or stage of life, for many 'christening' is something for babies. It goes hand-in-hand with the idea of confirmation, that when a child is old enough to speak for themselves, they can 'confirm' the baptismal vows made on their behalf by their parents and godparents.

Infant baptism is as much a cultural phenomenon as a religious one, which is partly why it has inspired a variety of thought about its merits. In the early church, baptism was for adults who professed faith in Jesus Christ, an additional dimension to that of John, who baptised 'for repentance', such that it was an act of initiation, the 'becoming' part of becoming a Christian. Once the Roman Empire became Christianised, in the early fourth century, whole households were baptised to mark their 'conversion' to Christianity. As subsequent babies were born they were baptised swiftly, not only to ensure that they became Christians as soon as possible (lest they might die as unbaptised heathens), but as an act of welcome into the family of faith.

A visit from the bishop was rare, so the idea of confirmation developed. On his arrival, the bishop would 'confirm' the baptisms that had already taken place months, or even years, previously. Rightly or wrongly, this is the tradition some churches have adopted and adapted ever since. It makes baptism a social as well as spiritual occasion, with much to celebrate in both dimensions.

The pandemic affected this as it did everything else. For children born in 2019 and early 2020, the 'natural' point of baptism was made difficult, if not impossible. While restrictions on numbers were imposed, they were not as draconian as those for weddings and funerals; nevertheless, for many baptism was deferred because of the much desired 'family gathering' aspect of a christening, and many churches later found themselves with a 'backlog'.

The social and cultural aspects of infant baptism give us pause for thought as to what is going on at a baptism. The journey from John the Baptist through Jesus, to the charge to the disciples to baptise in the name of the Trinity, remains strong and inspires us still. Baptism can be explained by the letters which make up the word; that is, baptism represents belonging, acceptance, protection, thanksgiving, integrity, sin and mystery.

When a child is born, they immediately *belong* to the family: parents, grandparents, siblings and the wider family of godparents and friends. They also belong to the family of the local church community into which they are welcomed. This means they are also members of the church of God, and that means they belong to God too. We belong to family, to each other, to the church and to God.

We *accept* this, and we accept who we are. We are lovely and loved people, caring but often damaged people. We make mistakes and get things wrong – we know that and accept that. God knows and accepts it too: God knows and loves us for who we are. We accept that with gratitude and grace.

We also ask God for *protection* for our little ones, to keep them safe, physically and spiritually. The world is not a safe place. People are in physical danger from diseases, natural disasters, violence, war and terror, and conspiracy theories and wicked words can harm people emotionally and spiritually. We all need protection, and at baptism we seek and wish it for babies from the outset.

Yet at the same time we also give *thanks* for the bundle of love and joy that a child is. We thank all those involved in the creation of new life and for safe delivery. This means thanking each other as well as thanking God.

Baptism, at any age, involves making vows and promises, and to do so demands *integrity*. For a baby, the parents and godparents make promises to each other and to God. Integrity is about meaning what we say and saying what we mean. Integrity is not to be assumed nor taken for granted in this world. Parents and godparents promise to bring up their child as a Christian. For this they need the help and grace of God, which is freely available. Yet in this, as in all things, we are all called to speak and act with integrity.

For baptism is all about *sin*. It is a dirty three-letter word we do not often hear these days, but we all know what it means. Baptism is about washing away sin: the sinful nature of humanity and the sins we commit past, present and future. We all behave badly sometimes, and in Jesus Christ there is the cleansing of this badness, of the stain it leaves on us and those whom we love. Likewise, we are all born separated from God – and separation from God is an important definition of sin – and in baptism we reconnect and symbolically wash this sinful nature away in response to repentance.

For all of this, though, there is something very strange about baptism. All this talk of sin and water on a baby's head – or total immersion – is rather odd. It is a *mystery*, in which God's Holy Spirit comes among us and, through water, makes a person spiritually clean, ready for a dirty world. And the cleansing water sticks: that is the whole point. It is not rinsed away or diluted by sin or suffering or sensibility or senility. The sticky water of baptism lasts a lifetime and beyond.

Jesus, who was baptised at the Jordan and who commanded your disciples to do likewise, we praise and bless you for the family of faith into which you call and welcome us. As each day dawns, renew us with your Spirit, that we may live as those forgiven and freed in faith, hope and love. Amen

6 Weddings

On the third day there was a wedding in Cana of Galilee, and the mother of Jesus was there. Jesus and his disciples had also been invited to the wedding. When the wine gave out, the mother of Jesus said to him, 'They have no wine.' And Jesus said to her, 'Woman, what concern is that to you and to me? My hour has not yet come.' His mother said to the servants, 'Do whatever he tells you.' Now standing there were six stone water-jars for the Jewish rites of purification, each holding twenty or thirty gallons. Jesus said to them, 'Fill the jars with water.' And they filled them up to the brim. He said to them, 'Now draw some out, and take it to the chief steward.' So they took it. When the steward tasted the water that had become wine, and did not know where it came from (though the servants who had drawn the water knew), the steward called the bridegroom and said to him, 'Everyone serves the good wine first, and then the inferior wine after the guests have become drunk. But you have kept the good wine until now.' Jesus did this, the first of his signs, in Cana of Galilee, and revealed his glory; and his disciples believed in him.

JOHN 2:1–11

Couples getting married in church sometimes choose this passage of scripture as a reading, because it is referred to in the liturgy and, on the face of it, is all about a wedding. We have no idea who was getting married in Cana, and it would not have been like today, when only a select number of guests are invited. The whole village would expect to attend. Nowadays budgets are tight, and an extravagant wedding can cost a small fortune. A whole industry has grown up to relieve couples of their money, and some couples even employ a wedding planner to do the legwork on organising the big day. Yet in Cana, something very unplanned happened, something of which the hosts would have been deeply ashamed: they ran out of wine. Mary intercedes and Jesus comes to the rescue, making something else unplanned happen: water becomes wine.

For any couple, something going wrong at their wedding is stressful indeed, and speaking as someone who has been involved in many weddings, it is notable how much care and attention goes into working out what happens where and when on a wedding day. Nevertheless my wife has always had a good word of advice for couples worrying about timings and itineraries and speeches and traffic: 'It can't go wrong; it can only go differently.' As a vicar, I could write at length about things which have 'gone differently' at weddings and the personalities involved. I will spare you that, but rather say that weddings are a joy and a privilege to be a part of.

During the pandemic period, weddings were variously forbidden, restricted in scope or limited in number. Some couples had their banns read only to have their nuptials banned. Many weddings were therefore postponed, sometimes more than once. It was a difficult time, and some companies involved in the wedding industry tried to penalise couples who had to postpone their weddings because of Covid. Even if they relented there was still the difficulty of finding alternative dates. Some couples opted for small-scale events, while others felt that having the 'big day' with lots of guests and a large party was very much part of the sense of occasion and value of the gathering. Strictly speaking, a couple only needs two witnesses and a minister (as registrar) to marry. Weddings often draw lots of people from different families and locations together, so there were particular risks where the spread of infection was concerned.

Much of this is icing on the cake, however. The key thing about a wedding, which is very much the key to the story of the wedding at

Cana, is change. Two people *change* into a couple, joined together, rings exchanged as tokens, before family and friends, who are right behind them as they commit the rest of their lives together to each other and, if in church, to God.

Change is inevitable and it can be difficult. Not everyone is able to embrace it, and it can cause much stress and anxiety; it can even contribute to death. Research indicates that the top ten most stressful life events are, in descending order: the death of a spouse; the death of a child; divorce; marital separation; imprisonment; the death of a close family member; personal injury or illness; getting married; dismissal from work; retirement. Moving house can be very stressful too, often compounded by being precipitated by one of the other events in the list. Although it's usually a happy event, getting married is nonetheless stressful. Some couples find organising the wedding stressful: it can test family relationships and presumptions, and the emphasis can fall on 'the wedding' rather than the marriage itself.

The story of Jesus changing water into wine is a happy event marking change, not only for the couple but also for Jesus himself. Jesus changes water into wine to symbolise that he is going to change everything and everyone. The water in the jars was for washing feet (something with which he would conclude his earthly ministry), but the wine just got better and better. This was and still is a positive change, which made everything different, for all eternity. It was all part of the plan: God's 'wedding plan' for the redemption of Israel and the whole world, with a new kind of relationship being formed with and through Jesus Christ.

John calls the turning of water into wine the first 'sign' by which Jesus revealed his glory. It is one of the great 'revealings' that is celebrated in the period after Epiphany. The magi, who represent the Gentiles coming to pay homage (Matthew 2), experience a revealing of God in the baby Jesus, as do Simeon and Anna in the temple (Luke 2). Similarly when Jesus is baptised by John (Matthew 3), this is also a sign that he has come into the world and that, by the Holy Spirit, glorious changes are presaged.

Furthermore, the water and wine remind us of the Eucharist and of Christ's blood spilled on the cross: 'One of the soldiers pierced his side with a spear, and at once blood and water came out' (John 19:34).

The changes that Jesus brings about in our lives need not be stressful, but they can be significant. Rather like marriage, they can appear stressful, as the call of Jesus is a call to believe differently, behave differently and belong to the world differently. Similarly, getting married requires a new and different self-perception, behaviour and sense of belonging, to the community and to each other. To welcome Christ into one's life is to embark upon and embrace a new relationship, and marriage makes a good model for that. By the same token, our relationship with Christ can also be a model for marital relationships, for both kinds of relationship can be founded on faith, hope and love. We learn how to love one another by loving and being loved by God; and we can learn to love God by loving one another.

O God, who in Jesus Christ calls us to be your faithful people, help us to adapt to the stresses and changes in our lives, to see them as signposts for growth in faith, strengthening of hope and opportunities for love. As Jesus changed water into wine, change us from glory to glory, till in heaven we take our place. Amen

Ascensiontide

7 Funerals

> So when they had come together, they asked him, 'Lord, is this the time when you will restore the kingdom to Israel?' He replied, 'It is not for you to know the times or periods that the Father has set by his own authority. But you will receive power when the Holy Spirit has come upon you; and you will be my witnesses in Jerusalem, in all Judea and Samaria, and to the ends of the earth.' When he had said this, as they were watching, he was lifted up, and a cloud took him out of their sight. While he was going and they were gazing up towards heaven, suddenly two men in white robes stood by them. They said, 'Men of Galilee, why do you stand looking up towards heaven? This Jesus, who has been taken up from you into heaven, will come in the same way as you saw him go into heaven.'
>
> ACTS 1:6–11

One of the harshest realities of the first stages of the Covid-19 pandemic was the speed with which someone could descend from having only mild symptoms to needing a ventilator – and sadly, in many thousands of cases, to death, unable to be saved by medical staff who risked their own health to help. In some cases, people who were rushed to hospital after catching the virus were never seen alive again, and those left at home were often paralysed by fear – of the unknown, of whether they would soon catch the virus, of what would happen next. Realising their partner, parent or child could die, many people turned to prayer. These victims were not statistics; they were real people who a week previously had no idea what was coming.

Often there was no chance to visit, say goodbye, hold a hand or pray with the dying patient. For many it was overwhelming, and we saw this shock and pain on our television screens every evening for a year. Then, when someone had died, whether of the virus or not, it was not possible to have a proper funeral. Only a few people could be present at a brief ceremony, while others were told it was not safe to attend. As a vicar in Enfield and after moving to Medway in Kent, I led some of these funerals. While they were intimate and subdued, their small scale added insult to injury for so many.

This was the reality of 2020 and 2021 for so many, and it is not so unlike the reality of that other story we might recall, of Jesus being arrested in the garden of Gethsemane, dragged off without ceremony or conversation, betrayed by a kiss, accused, tried, beaten, tried again, flogged and crucified. It was dangerous to be nearby; only those women who felt brave enough – and loyal enough – to stay kept watch as Jesus' life ebbed away, struggling for breath, stretched on the cross.

While the circumstances of those who have lost loved ones to Covid (or any quick-acting disease or sudden death) and those of the disciples 2,000 years ago are completely different, there is common emotional and psychological ground: hard, tear-stained, cold ground. Furthermore, Jesus was buried swiftly, by Nicodemus and Joseph; there is no record of anyone else being present or of any ritual or prayers, and certainly no eulogy. It is likely that some Jewish prayer for the dead would have been muttered, but the fact is Jesus had no funeral.

This is where the ascension comes in. Coming 40 days after his resurrection, the ascension is the closest thing to a funeral that Jesus had. That period of 40 days between Easter and ascension – during which amazing, unique, unbelievable, joyous things happened – teaches us the difference between goodbye and farewell (even though the Oxford English Dictionary describes them as interchangeable).

'Goodbye' is a contraction of 'God be with you', which ironically is how we often begin acts of worship – 'The Lord be with you.' The 'good' in 'goodbye' does not simply mean something pleasant; it refers to God. To say 'goodbye' to someone is to send them away with God. This is what happens at every funeral: an opportunity, in usual time at least, to say thank you and goodbye.

'Farewell' has a slightly different origin. While it may be a noun now – as in the musical piece the 'Ashokan Farewell' – it originates in something said to one going on a journey, an expression of the wish that they fare, or go, well. 'Farewell' has a sense of expectation of a reunion. The hymnwriter Jeremiah Rankin put it like this in 1880:

Till we meet, till we meet,
Till we meet at Jesus' feet;
Till we meet, till we meet,
God be with you till we meet again.

In Shakespeare's *Romeo and Juliet*, before Juliet takes her poison she says, 'Farewell! God knows when we shall meet again' – the implication being that they will, indeed, meet again. 'Goodbye', on the contrary, has a greater sense of finality and recognises the implicit, perhaps unspoken, possibility that the goodbye could be final. It is this inability to say final goodbyes that have crushed so many amid all too swift and sudden death from the coronavirus.

At Jesus' ascension, there is a sense of farewell, rather than goodbye. The disciples had to wait to say farewell and went through an emotional roller coaster between the crucifixion and the resurrection. Yet, at the end, there they were, looking to heaven, joyful in the realisation that this was not goodbye, but farewell. Jesus was journeying to the Father, to be united with God as he always had been and always would be, but he was going to return by sending the Holy Spirit, a divine dimension to dwell with them – and us – for good. It was a parting gift that took ten days to arrive. It gave them hope and joy.

It can give us hope and joy, too, if we remember that this farewell on the Jerusalem hillside, in sight of where Jesus had died and risen, is a promise of eternal presence and resurrection hope for all generations. It enables us to say goodbye to loved ones in a spirit of farewell – the spirit that tells us from deep within, that death is not the end.

Father God, whose son Jesus Christ met a sudden and painful death, isolated from friends and family, amid a flurry of activity unbearable to behold, have mercy on all who are close to death and hear the prayers of those who have lost their loved ones. Give them comfort in their sorrow, hope in their despair and light in the darkness of grief. Amen

Pentecost

8 Arts and crafts

The Lord spoke to Moses: See, I have called by name Bezalel son of Uri son of Hur, of the tribe of Judah: and I have filled him with divine spirit, with ability, intelligence, and knowledge in every kind of craft, to devise artistic designs, to work in gold, silver, and bronze, in cutting stones for setting, and in carving wood, in every kind of craft. Moreover, I have appointed with him Oholiab son of Ahisamach, of the tribe of Dan; and I have given skill to all the skilful, so that they may make all that I have commanded you: the tent of meeting, and the ark of the covenant, and the mercy-seat that is on it, and all the furnishings of the tent, the table and its utensils, and the pure lampstand with all its utensils, and the altar of incense, and the altar of burnt-offering with all its utensils, and the basin with its stand, and the finely worked vestments, the holy vestments for the priest Aaron and the vestments of his sons, for their service as priests, and the anointing-oil and the fragrant incense for the holy place. They shall do just as I have commanded you.

EXODUS 31:1–11

While the lockdowns of 2020 and 2021 were mostly unwelcome, some people relished the 'free time' that had been imposed upon them. Many took to exercise, reading or doing some form of art or craft, such as painting, drawing, sculpture, sewing, woodwork – or even DIY, itself a form of skilled craft. According to a survey of 2,000 people conducted by Brother Sewing, a third of women aged 35 or over took up sewing or embroidery during lockdown, while among 25–34-year-olds more men took up sewing than women (23% compared to 21%). Remarkably the same survey reveals that more men aged 25–34 chose to sew rather than keep fit (20%), do gardening (13%) or learn a new language (15%). It also seems that only one in eight young men played computer games during this period. Where women over 65 are concerned, 43% said they started sewing over lockdown.

This may be because an act of craft produces a result – an object, a satisfying reward, or artifact that arises as a direct consequence of the activity. Craft is not a peripheral or isolated area of specialist interest, but is now firmly established in the mainstream. Similarly, we have developed an increased awareness of and desire for professionally made craftworks. Television programmes such as *The Great British Sewing Bee* and *The Great Pottery Throw Down* attract millions of viewers. Commercially, handicrafts have flourished with new routes to market with online craft purchases growing from 5% of buyers (332,000 people) in 2006 to 19% of buyers (3.2 million people) in 2010 to 33% of buyers (10.3 million people) in 2020.

While we may want to distinguish between 'arts' (painting, music, sculpture, literature) and 'crafts' (carving, shoemaking, carpentry), the distinction is a relatively modern one, which the ancient world would not recognise. The notion of the 'artist' is a modern phenomenon, fuelled by romanticism and affirmed by our modern cult of celebrity. The Greek word for art – or craft – is *techné*, from which we get the words technical, technique, technology and architecture. For Plato (c. 428–347 BC), a 'good' knife was a sharp one – one that cut well. As such, it was a reflection of the image of an 'ideal' knife – the perfect specimen to which all aspired and of which all actual knives were but shadowy replicas. A knife could look beautiful of course, but if it was blunt, it was useless and no good. What we might think of as artistic or aesthetic features were secondary. Of course, a good knife or shoe could look good too, and as the years have gone by the situation has reversed in some spheres, such that the aesthetic value of an object can be elevated above its practical value. Some very fine-looking shoes are very uncomfortable!

The Jewish tradition was a bit better at combining the need for beauty and function: Moses commanded the craftsmen to make finely worked vestments, using knowledge of every kind of craft, to work in precious metal and materials and 'devise artistic designs'. This amounts to a culture clash – a difference of philosophical opinion and approach between the ancient Greeks and Hebrews. To a great extent Christians have inherited aspects of both approaches, mostly from the apostle Paul, who was a classically educated Jew. We value arts and crafts, appreciating the aesthetic properties of objects which also serve a specific function. Consider whether, in a kitchen shop, the most expensive knives are the ones which look best, handle best, cut best or all three.

The creation of aesthetic objects (a term which covers works of both art and craft) is often associated with immortality. The poet Marcus Bruce Christian wrote that those who create true beauty live forever, a sentiment that resonates with how George Orwell thought of literature – a writer becomes immortal through their art; they live on in the works they create. The words of biblical writers and classical poets and playwrights still speak to us long after they have gone. Meanwhile, in ancient Greek culture, immortality was enshrined not so much in the stories that you *tell*, but the stories that are told *about you* after you are gone. Who has the greatest immortality: Homer, or Odysseus and Achilles?

It is the same with crafts: which lasts longer, the shoe or the shoemaker, the pot or the potter? It is perhaps no coincidence that shoemakers rely on a *last* to shape a shoe and go on making more shoes. The last, or mould, outlives the shoe and ensures the continuity of being able to make new shoes. The shoe (or tapestry, or dress, or lampstand) is made by a maker, lovingly, with skill and craft.

We have a creator, who has fashioned us intimately and knows every stitch, curve and contour of our perfectly conceived souls. Furthermore, we have a glimpse of our creator God whenever we strive to make anything ourselves. With our own hands, eyes, fingers and imagination, we conceive of something from nothing, or we copy something, and we put our minds and bodies to work. It yields something that is lasting, beautiful and satisfying to our creative desires. It is, as Plato might say, but a reflection of the true creative process, only the shadow of which we might see around us, but of which, in being creative ourselves, we have a sense. Just as our creative process is but a shadow of the divine, so too is the fractional immortality we obtain by leaving our works behind us for others to appreciate and remember us by.

God, by whose Spirit the universe has been crafted and humanity fashioned, we thank you for the gifts of creativity, skill and imagination with which you bless our lives. Through our handiwork help us see your greater power and beauty, until that day when the new creation is finished, and by the same Spirit we are brought into the realm of everlasting love, where you reign in unity as creator, redeemer and sustainer. Amen

Trinity

9 Books

I, John, your brother who share with you in Jesus the perse-cution and the kingdom and the patient endurance, was on the island called Patmos because of the word of God and the testimony of Jesus. I was in the spirit on the Lord's day, and I heard behind me a loud voice like a trumpet saying, 'Write in a book what you see and send it to the seven churches, to Ephesus, to Smyrna, to Pergamum, to Thyatira, to Sardis, to Philadelphia, and to Laodicea.'

Then I turned to see whose voice it was that spoke to me, and on turning I saw seven golden lampstands, and in the midst of the lampstands I saw one like the Son of Man, clothed with a long robe and with a golden sash across his chest. His head and his hair were white as white wool, white as snow; his eyes were like a flame of fire, his feet were like burnished bronze, refined as in a furnace, and his voice was like the sound of many waters. In his right hand he held seven stars, and from his mouth came a sharp, two-edged sword, and his face was like the sun shining with full force.

When I saw him, I fell at his feet as though dead. But he placed his right hand on me, saying, 'Do not be afraid; I am the first and the last, and the living one. I was dead, and see, I am alive forever and ever; and I have the keys of Death and of Hades. Now write what you have seen, what is, and what is to take place after this.

REVELATION 1:9–19

Many would say that to live in a world without books or literature in any form would be a disaster. As a civilisation we owe an incalculable amount to the written word, which, through ancient texts, manuscripts, bound volumes, paperbacks and e-readers has given us access to the thoughts of countless women and men who have influenced our way of life, beliefs and thinking. Histories, fiction, biographies, poetry, drama, instruction manuals, political ideologies and so much more have been published since the revolutionary invention of the printing press by Johannes Gutenberg in 1439.

The book he printed first was *the* book – the Bible – named after the Greek word for scrolls (*biblia*). The English word comes to us through Old English (*boc*) from an old Germanic word meaning 'beech', while the Latin word *codex* originates in the word for a block of wood, suggesting that the first 'books' were carved on wood, or perhaps had their 'leaves' bound between pieces of wood.

A second, equally powerful, shift in publishing came about with the beginnings of the World Wide Web in the 1980s, often attributed to Tim Berners-Lee: another publishing revolution which has changed the world through the branching out of the written word on to electronic devices.

Books can be dangerous as well as uplifting. While many provide entertainment, others have been banned, because it is obvious that one is influenced by what one reads. To kill an idea, burn the books, deny access to the webpages, destroy the technology. Whether a book is fact or fiction, disturbing or docile, it has power, as do plays and symphonies. Therefore dictatorships take a particular interest in all the arts, but especially literature. For books impart knowledge and opinion, and that is why the printing press could be one of the most significant inventions of all time. It undoubtedly facilitated the reformation in Europe, for what one reads affects how one prays, and what one prays determines what one believes (as in the Latin phrase, *lex orandi, lex credendi*). The prayer books of the reformation were *books*, and they changed Europe and her colonies forever.

During the 2020 lockdowns, when only 'essential' shops could remain open, bookshops had to close. As well as affecting the lives and livelihoods of booksellers, it begged the question as to whether a book is an 'essential' item. Sad as closing bookshops was, income from book sales in the UK rose by more than £100 million that year. According to the Publishers Association, 'the nation turned to books for comfort, escapism and relaxation' and 'reading triumphed, with adults and children alike reading more during lockdown than before'. Audio book sales rose by a third and fiction sales by 16%. Nevertheless, sales of printed books fell 6%, no doubt because the physical shops were closed. Digital sales of texts increased 12%. Overall this meant that in 2020 nearly half of 'book' sales were digital. This makes me wonder, as I write, whether what you are reading now, which originated on a screen, is being read on one.

Back in the apostle John's day, around 69 AD, when he was inspired to write his revelations down, as instructed by the trumpet-like voice, he took to parchment and wrote in Greek. Instructed to 'write in a book' and distribute it to the seven churches, he was told to 'publish' his visions abroad. This call to publication meant producing scrolls, to be read aloud to assembled congregations in those places, who would treat them as scripture. The same text would be read by different people in different places. Ultimately, John's Revelation became the final chapter of the best-ever selling book in the universe. Its place at the 'end' of the Bible was not fully determined until the 'canon' of scripture was settled in the fourth century, but Revelation was secure because of its widely accepted apostolic authorship. Unusual as it is, it did not come from what the commentator John Sweet called 'the lunatic fringe', and has its antecedents deep in the book of Daniel and other pre-Christian writings. Strange as it may seem, Revelation is very much part of the Christian tradition, and the injunction to 'publish' letters to churches falls very much within the norms of the first century, when none other than the apostle Paul was doing likewise.

It may have been thought that books would die out with the internet revolution. Not so, even if we turn our pages with a swipe, rather than a flick of a finger. The written word is a blessing, a comfort and a joy as well as a vehicle for emotion, reflection, teaching and prayer. As human beings, made in the image of the one who is Word incarnate, we uniquely possess a level of linguistic ability hitherto unknown, such that the mind is our tool, the word is our raw material and the book our delivery system. Next time you read or write a book, give thanks simply for the ability to do so and reflect on how God has spoken to you directly or tangentially by the written word.

O God, the author of all things, thank you for the gift of words by which we can gain access to the hidden meanings of your creation, your will and your salvation. Through him who is your Word made flesh, enable us to translate your words of life into actions of love, that reading, we may embrace and embody the gospel brought by the same Jesus Christ our Lord. Amen

10 Scripture

But as for you, continue in what you have learned and firmly believed, knowing from whom you learned it, and how from childhood you have known the sacred writings that are able to instruct you for salvation through faith in Christ Jesus. All scripture is inspired by God and is useful for teaching, for reproof, for correction, and for training in righteousness, so that everyone who belongs to God may be proficient, equipped for every good work.

In the presence of God and of Christ Jesus, who is to judge the living and the dead, and in view of his appearing and his kingdom, I solemnly urge you: proclaim the message; be persistent whether the time is favourable or unfavourable; convince, rebuke, and encourage, with the utmost patience in teaching.

2 TIMOTHY 3:14—4:2

One of the major phenomena of musical performance in recent years has been the widespread attempt to perform music 'authentically'. Performers of Mozart have tried, and have tried to justify, performing his music 'the way he would have intended it to be heard' or 'how it would have been heard by his contemporaries'. This has involved using musical instruments of the period, genuine or copied. The results are fascinating and provoke questions as to whether the resulting performances are 'better'. Bach and Beethoven did not have pianos as we know them, so performances sound different, and the sound of a modern piano might have been horrible or delightful to these composers. We will never know. We might also wonder if it matters whether they would like it – perhaps the most 'authentic' performances of pieces of music are those which speak from the heart of the music itself through the heart of the performer to the heart and mind of the listener. How the music is played might be more important than what instrument it is played on.

The fact that such an enterprise cannot be verified (there is no one to ask) connects the playing of music on obsolete instruments with any enterprise that draws on historical insight and knowledge. This includes the reading and interpretation of literature. We cannot ask Shakespeare what he meant, and some would say it does not matter; what matters is what his work means to us today. This is why so many performances of his plays seek to 'translate' the plot into a modern setting, or indeed any setting: *Romeo and Juliet* set in outer space or *Henry V* in World War II period costume. *Julius Caesar* can be performed in any age, because themes of power, rebellion, war and betrayal are always with us. This is one of the profound delights to be found in the timelessness of great literature and drama.

As a form of literature, scripture is likewise timeless and, on another level, inaccessible. The technical name for this paradox is hermeneutics: the study of how to equate the world of the time of writing with the world in which we live and move and have our being. It becomes important when considering how to respond to some of Paul's teachings – for example, about women, sexuality, food or leadership. Paul lived in an age very different from ours, and it is not always easy to unravel the significance of his context as a reflection of the divine word implanted in him by the Holy Spirit of God.

Yet with Paul himself we can say that 'all scripture is inspired by God'. We can also say that the themes of scripture: creation, sin, salvation, faith, hope and love are timeless, relevant in any day and age. Scripture speaks to us of a God who is unchanging, whose creative power, redeeming love and spiritual presence are fixed points in an ever-changing, fragile world. That such a statement can be made is also testimony to part of the purpose of scripture: to enable us to understand the world from a divine perspective, to glimpse the eternal and ground it in our daily lives.

The daily task of reading scripture brings with it therefore the daily question of how it is relevant to me today. The German theologian Dietrich Bonhoeffer, who was executed by the Nazis a few days before the war ended in 1945, asked a similar question of his students at Finkenwalde Seminary – 'Who is Jesus Christ, for us, today?' For him, in his day, the answer to both questions involved a calling to be a participant in plots to overthrow Adolf Hitler, advocating even his death. His view was that to remain silent was effectively to condone, and not to take action was an act in itself.

Bonhoeffer also said that Christians are very good at reading the Bible *for* ourselves, but less good at reading the Bible *against* ourselves. When Wycliffe and Luther and Tyndale and Coverdale translated the Bible, they did not do it so that we could make of it what we will and use it to defend whatever we want to believe. Far from it: the Bible is a dangerous and challenging book, and that is why for centuries its text was inaccessible to the people of God. Sometimes the Bible tells us to do things, to believe things and to handle life and others in ways we do not like. The Bible is a book against which we might judge ourselves and, inevitably, others. It is easy to forget that the majority of Christians did not have access to scriptural texts for the first 1,500 years of Christianity.

Today, we can not only access the Bible on our phones and read it whenever we wish, we can also look back and consider how our forebears read it. In our present reading, from 2 Timothy, there is a sense of the past, as we consider how the words of divinely inspired scripture landed in different places and different times. Different groups of people emphasised different aspects; or rather different voices in the Bible spoke to them in diverse contexts. Whether formerly enslaved populations; different genders; victims of oppression, abuse, terror and war; capitalists, Marxists or environmentalists: all read the Bible for themselves, and sometimes against themselves or against society.

It is not that we, or they, can make the Bible mean what they want it to, but rather that God speaks into every situation, and scripture is still heard in every age. The Bible has plenty to say to us about living through a coronavirus pandemic, even though there are no direct references to Covid-19 in its pages. Nor could, would or should there be, and to say so would be to treat the Bible as something it is not: something which can be changed or which is located solely in the time and context in which its various chapters were written.

The purpose of scripture, says Paul, is twofold: so that we may be 'instructed for salvation' and so that we may be 'proficiently equipped for good works'. These goals have never changed, and they reflect the inner and outer workings of the Holy Spirit in Christian lives, revealed in faith and work. We need both, and the Bible is our living source book – always has been and always will be.

Creator God, who has written the volume of history with a loving pen and imbued the human story with freedom and knowledge, thank you for the gift of holy scripture to lead, guide and sustain us in this and every age. May we be always drawn to its pages of peace, chapters of truth and words of wisdom, which point to and are revealed in Jesus Christ, the Word made flesh. Amen

11 Recharging

Answer me when I call, O God of my right!
　　You gave me room when I was in distress.
　　Be gracious to me, and hear my prayer.

How long, you people, shall my honour suffer shame?
　　How long will you love vain words, and seek after lies?
But know that the Lord has set apart the faithful for himself;
　　the Lord hears when I call to him.

When you are disturbed, do not sin;
　　ponder it on your beds, and be silent.
Offer right sacrifices,
　　and put your trust in the Lord.

There are many who say, 'O that we might see some good!
　　Let the light of your face shine on us, O Lord!'
You have put gladness in my heart
　　more than when their grain and wine abound.

I will both lie down and sleep in peace;
　　for you alone, O Lord, make me lie down in safety.
PSALM 4

On 14 December 1998, I appeared on the front page of *The Times*, with the headline 'Canon offers a blessing of mobile phones'. I had published an article online in which someone 'married' their phone, promising to stick together through thick and thin. As Ruth Gledhill of *The Times* put it:

Although it is a satirical liturgy which clearly lacks the *gravitas* of standard church fare, it is intended to illustrate a serious point represented by the advance of new technologies. The service opens with 'We have come together in the presence of God to ask God's succour and support in the management, use and care of this mobile telephonic apparatus.'

The article caused a bit of a stir, and I found myself on BBC Radio Four's *Today* programme that morning. In 1998 it was controversial to suggest that we would become wedded to our mobile phones. Now, no one would dare disagree.

The first cell phones were the size of bricks and in frequent need of recharging. For a long time, Nokia was the leading mass producer of mobile phones, and then in January 2007 Apple announced the first of a succession of iPhones. Not everyone has a smartphone, of course, although there are around 6.5 billion of them, and another billion 'unsmart' phones. The widespread manufacture, use and disposal of mobile phones is an ecological issue, with many containing precious and scarce metals. The smartphone is a 21st-century phenomenon, although the first mobile telephone is reckoned to be the one made by Motorola in 1973.

Mobile phones need to be charged and, like human beings, most of them do not last a whole day without needing a rest, either plugged into the wall or lying on a flat bed, recharging wirelessly for new life and activity. It is perhaps no coincidence that many people charge their phones overnight, by the side of the bed even. Their phones sleep while they do and rise with them in the morning, fully charged and ready for all those emails, photos, videos, social media posts and text messages.

We all need recharging and often use the language of energy drain in reference to our own lives. A retreat or quiet day can be an opportunity to take time out and 'recharge' our spiritual 'batteries'. After stressful periods in life or relentless busy times, we can often feel 'drained', 'flat' or that we have 'run out of steam'. These are all meta-phors of power supply and, for sure, we all need energy, and we all run out of it from time to time.

The Covid-19 pandemic drained us all. Many emerged from it tired, but they had to keep going. Being locked down at home is not nec-essarily relaxing or a chance to rejuvenate, and many key workers and others have slogged their way through recent years and are still working flat out. The psychological, mental and spiritual impact of this continues to be felt. We have taken to using technology even more extensively, which can also be draining. As well as distancing us socially from our colleagues, family and friends, it can be tiring on the eyes and can create a sense of being constantly available, of living a life that has no downtime, no recharging opportunity. As the US Federal Communications Commission put it: 'To reduce their harmful effects, one should always remember that a mobile phone is a friend, not a master, and it should never be used too much'. As we move forward, we need to be careful that the habits we formed during the pandemic lockdowns do not become normative, because relentless availability, screen time and blurred edges between work and social life can be damaging and soul-destroying.

Although writing so long ago, the psalmist seems to understand this when he writes: 'You gave me room when I was in distress. Be gracious to me, and hear my prayer.' He gives advice: 'The Lord hears when I call to him. When you are disturbed, do not sin; ponder it on your beds, and be silent.'

There can be too much reflectiveness, or the wrong sort, and the pandemic has caused some to dwell on their troubles, to resent con-finement and to struggle to relate to others. Many people have had good reason to be morose, but it damages mental well-being signifi-cantly. There is much care and prayer needed for those who are still struggling to emerge from the dark days of isolation, bereavement and shock. We have lived through a period of sudden, lonely deaths, suppressed grief and fear. So many died, but many more have had close encounters with their own mortality and have been on the knife edge of life and death. This saps energy and well-being.

Yet many turned to prayer, and by quiet contemplation we can reflect well in the presence of God, from whom we have never needed to maintain any distance. Indeed, many have come spiritually close to God during times of social distancing. Churches may have been closed for a while, but God did not desert us; God remained accessible for wireless recharging throughout. As the psalmist concludes his meditation on handling stress: 'I will both lie down and sleep in peace; for you alone, O Lord, make me lie down in safety.'

Such safety is never to be taken for granted, and we may feel that some prayers have not been answered as loved ones have suffered and died at home and abroad. That itself merits deep reflection in the presence of God, and for that we need spiritual energy as well as trust and faith. For the spiritual charger is always there, at home, in church, among friends, and is often found by the bed: so we can rest in the Lord. As the psalmist also put it: 'I lie down and sleep; I wake again, for the Lord sustains me' (Psalm 3:5).

When you lie down to sleep, offer the energy spent to God and seek his renewing, spiritual power to enter the coming day recharged with faith, hope and love.

God of power and might, you surrendered your strength to take human form, emptying yourself that we may be saved. Renew us your servants in faith and hope, that we may feel your loving mercy working among us, that we may be enlightened, enlivened and encouraged this and every day. Amen

Summer

12 Bicycle relay

Now I should remind you, brothers and sisters, of the good news that I proclaimed to you, which you in turn received, in which also you stand, through which also you are being saved, if you hold firmly to the message that I proclaimed to you – unless you have come to believe in vain.

For I handed on to you as of first importance what I in turn had received: that Christ died for our sins in accordance with the scriptures, and that he was buried, and that he was raised on the third day in accordance with the scriptures, and that he appeared to Cephas, then to the twelve. Then he appeared to more than five hundred brothers and sisters at one time, most of whom are still alive, though some have died. Then he appeared to James, then to all the apostles. Last of all, as to one untimely born, he appeared also to me. For I am the least of the apostles, unfit to be called an apostle, because I persecuted the church of God. But by the grace of God I am what I am, and his grace towards me has not been in vain.

1 CORINTHIANS 15:1–10A

In June and July 2021, the Cathedrals Cycle Route challenge took to the highways and byways of England. Setting out from Newcastle, they headed south, in a variety of weathers, through York, down to London, where they did the shortest leg, between St Paul's and Southwark, and then followed the ancient pilgrimage route from London to Canterbury via Rochester before turning west, heading to Truro,

and then back up the country through Worcester, wending their way to Carlisle and then back to Newcastle. While only one person, Shaun Cutler, did the whole 2,000-mile route, the challenge lasted 42 days and took in all of England's 42 cathedrals.

As well as being a great feat of teamwork, the event was an opportunity to reflect upon physical and mental well-being and a great way to bring people together after so long a series of lockdowns. It being a relay rather than a race, the lead rider carried a baton, which was handed on from cathedral to cathedral. It was a beautiful baton, made from bronze to a design by Shaun's 13-year-old daughter. It featured two sculptured hands reaching towards each other, symbolising the idea that 'some days you need a hand, other days you are called to lend a hand'.

The baton was literally handed over at each cathedral; prayers were said on arrival and departure and a special candle lit for the remaining days of the cycle pilgrimage. Rather like the Olympic torch, this baton travelled the length and breadth of the country and, although no light travelled, it was already present at each destination, symbolising the light of Christ countrywide, renewed in the hand of friendship and fellowship across the miles. This was particularly poignant as the country cautiously opened up, and these cyclists, joining in for various parts of the route, travelled further on their bikes than they had done for many a month by road or rail.

Not everyone rides a bike, although by now there are more than a billion in existence. This is equivalent to the number of cars, and in many places they are the main mode of transport. In richer countries they are leisure vehicles, valued for cardiovascular fitness and well-being. During the Covid-19 lockdowns, the UK government encouraged cycling and provided vouchers for people to get their bikes roadworthy, and there was a global shortage of bikes as the world woke up to their health, financial and ecological benefits.

The bicycle's origin can be traced to Mannheim in 1817, where a pedal-less contraption appeared. Various other improvements were subsequently developed, including the famous penny farthing. The bike as we know it appeared in 1885 – the Rover safety bicycle, which had chain-driven, rear-wheel drive and similar-sized wheels. Two years later a pneumatic rubber tyre made by Dunlop was added, and we have been riding the same kind of bike ever since.

With the exception of tandems, a bicycle is a solo affair on which we ride our own journeys. Nevertheless people often ride in groups, and this is what the Cathedrals Cycle Route challenge was all about: a fellowship of the road; a solitary activity, socially distanced, but in tandem with others, with a common motive, route and point of arrival. So added to the dimension of relay, of handing on the baton, there is the dimension of 'church', of faithful people doing something individual, together. A group of cyclists is known as a peloton, and the group saves energy by riding close to each other, reducing drag significantly. In races this becomes a complex nexus of tactics among teams and riders, whereas in leisure cycling it is a form of cooperation. Riders look out for their neighbours on the journey. For we are all on the same journey, to the same destination, travelling singly, together.

The life of faith is like a relay. The apostle Paul once said that he 'fought the good fight… finished the race… kept the faith' (2 Timothy 4:7). His words to the Corinthians about the resurrection are in the same vein, and truly give us a picture of the sense Paul had of being part of a chain, a baton holder, handing on truth and tradition in a relay of faith. John the Baptist had the same idea when he met Jesus at the Jordan and, after baptising him, declared, 'You yourselves are my witnesses that I said, "I am not the Messiah, but I have been sent ahead of him"… He must increase, but I must decrease' (John 3:28, 30). The church has taken a similar view ever since, for however we understand revolutions and reformations, religious reactions and renewals, at the core of them all lies the transmission and transference of the truth of the Christian gospel, interpreted, retold and *handed on* afresh.

Paul handed on to us, via the Corinthian community of Christians, two important batons of belief. The first he mentions is the Eucharist:

> For I received from the Lord what I also handed on to you, that the Lord Jesus on the night when he was betrayed took a loaf of bread, and when he had given thanks, he broke it and said, 'This is my body that is for you. Do this in remembrance of me.'
> 1 CORINTHIANS 11:23–24

Then a little later he reminds them of what he has already 'handed on' – the basics of belief, that Jesus was handed over to be crucified, died and rose again, appearing to the disciples, at the end of which chain Paul places himself as last and least. The same thread extends to us this very day, a continuous relay race of faith, hope and love, handed on by our spiritual mothers and fathers from one generation to another.

Jesus, you have revealed yourself through the Holy Spirit to each and every generation; give us grace to receive you in bread and wine, and to hand on the truth of your resurrection to those with whom we ride on the journey of faith, hope and love. Amen

13 Zoom

If I speak in the tongues of mortals and of angels, but do not have love, I am a noisy gong or a clanging cymbal. And if I have prophetic powers, and understand all mysteries and all knowledge, and if I have all faith, so as to remove mountains, but do not have love, I am nothing. If I give away all my possessions, and if I hand over my body so that I may boast, but do not have love, I gain nothing.

Love is patient; love is kind; love is not envious or boastful or arrogant or rude. It does not insist on its own way; it is not irritable or resentful; it does not rejoice in wrongdoing, but rejoices in the truth. It bears all things, believes all things, hopes all things, endures all things.

Love never ends. But as for prophecies, they will come to an end; as for tongues, they will cease; as for knowledge, it will come to an end. For we know only in part, and we prophesy only in part; but when the complete comes, the partial will come to an end. When I was a child, I spoke like a child, I thought like a child, I reasoned like a child; when I became an adult, I put an end to childish ways. For now we see in a mirror, dimly, but then we will see face to face. Now I know only in part; then I will know fully, even as I have been fully known. And now faith, hope, and love abide, these three; and the greatest of these is love.

1 CORINTHIANS 13

When I was a vicar in North London, I produced a bookmark for each member of the congregation which was distributed at a family service

as part of the all-age talk. Entitled 'Gordon's guide to growing with God', and laid out vertically as an A–Z, it went like this:

> Always pray, Believe and behave, Consider others, Discern the deeds of the devil, Enjoy each and every day, Follow Christ, Glorify God, Help all people, Invest time in others, Just say 'Jesus is Lord', Keep the sabbath, Love your neighbour, Make enemies friends, Never give up, Open your heart to God, Prepare to die, Quieten your spirit, Remember the rules, Shun sin, Thank God, Unburden your soul, View violence as vile, Worship together, eXamine your life, Yield your will, Zoom in to God.

Several years later, Covid-19 struck and a member of the congregation, Julia, reminded me of the smart little bookmark and its yet-to-be ironic final line, 'Zoom in to God.' For by then we had found ourselves unable to go to church to 'worship together' and the idea of 'preparing to die' was no joke. 'Helping all people', 'examining our lives' and 'always praying' were serendipitous too. Which is to say that these basic phrases of faith came into their own during the pandemic.

In particular, the online platform Zoom was becoming a household name, much used by churches and home groups as well as businesses. Other providers are available, created by the major technology companies, such as Microsoft and Google, but just as the company Hoover became inextricably connected with the vacuum cleaner, Zoom has become a generic verb, whether one 'zooms' on Zoom, Teams or any other interactive online platform. Covid-19 changed our working and domestic lives overnight, and Zoom caught up extremely quickly: so swiftly that the company, which charges businesses while providing limited free use for the general public, saw sales soar 326% to US$2.6 billion in 2020 overall. A 40% increase was predicted the following year, taking the turnover to more than US$3.7 billion. Such growth may not continue at the same rate now, but Eric Yuan, who founded Zoom in 2011, says working from home is here to stay.

Zoom mirrors our imperfect attempts to relate to one another. The computer screen is a dark glass through which we see only dimly, if at all, and as a medium of communication it does not enable us to display or recognise emotions freely. Seeing someone's face and their lips move is not the same as being with them, although during lockdowns it was better than not communicating at all. The poor substitute that Zoom and its siblings have provided has been both a godsend and a stark reminder that this is not how we are truly meant to relate to one another or to God.

Some have applauded the way the church jumped on the Zoom band-wagon and made the most of it, and some people have even said that they prefer worship or fellowship from home, in their pyjamas, coffee in one hand and mouse in the other, and that geographical, even lin-guistic boundaries are transcended by this technology. It has enabled some people to re-engage with the life of the church, of which their health, well-being or mobility had deprived them. On the other hand, others have missed face-to-face fellowship and family gatherings, which a family Zoom quiz night could never replace.

It is all true, not an either/or, but the advent of Zoom reminds us of the impartial, the imperfect, the incomplete. It reflects the poverty of human faith, hope and love. For there is greater love, deeper faith and better hope than that which we experience amid the gloom of earthly life, manifested and anticipated in Jesus Christ. The apostle Paul used the metaphor of a mirror, which in his day would have been a polished piece of metal or at best the newly invented technique of fixing lead on the back of glass. So Paul's mirrors were no better than a Zoom call fragmented by a shaky internet connection.

Zoom mirrors reality, literally putting left on the right side, and it is neither real nor adequate compared to the glory that is yet to revealed. As Paul put it to another church community in Rome:

> I consider that the sufferings of this present time are not worth comparing with the glory about to be revealed to us. For the

creation waits with eager longing for the revealing of the children of God; for the creation was subjected to futility, not of its own will but by the will of the one who subjected it, in hope that the creation itself will be set free from its bondage to decay and will obtain the freedom of the glory of the children of God.

ROMANS 8:18–21

Next time you are on a video call, or hear about one, give thanks for technology and the partial gifts and pleasures it affords. But also be reminded of the greater hope and deeper faith into which our adversities call us and the perfect love which will come only through face-to-face encounter with our Lord and Saviour Jesus Christ.

God, whose face we see but dimly in human life, by your Holy Spirit, help us to focus on our faith, that we may handle our hope with grace, and live in the love you reveal uniquely in Jesus Christ, your Son, our Lord. Amen

14 Church music

Above all, clothe yourselves with love, which binds everything together in perfect harmony. And let the peace of Christ rule in your hearts, to which indeed you were called in the one body. And be thankful. Let the word of Christ dwell in you richly; teach and admonish one another in all wisdom; and with gratitude in your hearts sing psalms, hymns, and spiritual songs to God. And whatever you do, in word or deed, do everything in the name of the Lord Jesus, giving thanks to God the Father through him.

COLOSSIANS 3:14–17

No churchgoer can have failed to notice the absence of singing during the pandemic. It was greatly missed, and alongside its absence came a demoralising deprivation of activity for those engaged in church music, many of whom were unemployed or on furlough for over a year. The musical profession was one of the hardest hit by the prevention of communal activities.

Not having hymns in church has been salutary and instructive. Choirs accustomed to singing together regularly lost not only a pattern and purpose of life but part of their social nexus and, very likely, some ability. Church choirs which include children found themselves almost starting again from scratch when corporate singing finally became permissible. The rebooting of choirs was a challenge of finance, talent, discipline and commitment. So much music was lost.

The history of music in worship does not see its absence as universally bad. In fact, when we consider how important music has been

and still is to every society, it is quite remarkable how infrequently it is mentioned in the Bible. The first musician was Jubal (Genesis 4:21), whose name may be derived from the Hebrew word for 'ram', suggesting he played a ram's horn (*shofar*), an ancient instrument used in Jewish worship. Psalms was the Jewish hymn book and while only some psalms were written by David, he gained a reputation as the archetypal musician, portrayed throughout history with a lyre or harp. Once the temple was established at Jerusalem, professional musicians intoned the chants and the congregation responded. Everything was sung from memory.

Meanwhile, in ancient Greece, Plato felt it necessary to point out that music could be dangerous because of its ability to take over the consciousness of listeners. He proposed that everyone in the community should 'voice always one and the same sentiment in song, story and speech' (*Laws* ii, 664a). Music could be dangerous, but could also guide others in political and religious matters. The contrast between Hebrew and Greek attitudes towards music is noticeable, and these two strands meet in the first-century Middle East.

We know that singing God's praise was in vogue when Jesus was born: the angels sang 'Glory to God!' and shepherds heard them (Luke 2:13–14). At the other end of his earthly life, Jesus and the disciples sang a hymn together before going out to the garden of Gethsemane (Mark 14:26), just as they would have done had they been at the synagogue. Paul commends hymn singing and music in the context of worship: 'When you come together, each one has a hymn, a lesson, a revelation, a tongue, or an interpretation. Let all things be done for building up' (1 Corinthians 14:26). He also describes himself as one who sings: 'I will sing praise with the spirit, but I will sing praise with the mind also' (1 Corinthians 14:15). Yet where music was aligned with pagan religion, there was a problem, and the musical world of Corinth was likely beset with musicians involved in sorcery and idolatry. Equally problematic was the attitude of the Romans, who held that music was basically for entertainment. Both Greek and Roman attitudes confronted and influenced the ancient and reverential Jewish view on music in worship.

Augustine helped make music acceptable in the early church, saying, 'We are urged to sing to the Lord a new song. It is a new person who sings a new song. A song is a joyful thing, and if we reflect more deeply, it is also a matter of love… a new person will both sing a new song and belong to the new covenant.' A thousand years later, Martin Luther took up the cause: 'It was not without reason that the fathers and prophets wanted nothing else to be associated as closely with the Word of God as music. Therefore, we have so many hymns and Psalms where message and music join to move the listener's soul, while in other living beings and [sounding] bodies music remains a language without words.'

Many miles away in Geneva, John Calvin took a less enthusiastic, but by no means negative, line. Over in Zurich, though, Ulrich Zwingli, who was an accomplished singer and player of no less than the lute, harp, viols, flute, trumpet, dulcimer and waldhorn, felt that music was a source of pleasure and recreation, to be separated from religion, faith and worship, and notoriously banned it from church. Having lost church music for over a year, we now have a sense of what that must have been like. Zwingli's opinion did not prevail for much more than 50 years after his death, in battle, in 1531.

Later theologians, including Friedrich Schleiermacher, have helped us see music and religious feeling as closely related. The idea that music can transport us to a non-intellectual realm, communicating where words fail, is an appealing one, and Schleiermacher's emphasis and defence of music's ineffability is still popular, heavily influenced as it is by a prevailing, contemporaneous strand of Romanticism. For him, the very fact that music is not a referential or representational artform enables it to express the kind of wordless stirrings that characterise religious experience.

One of Schleiermacher's greatest successors was Karl Barth, who famously suggested that in heaven the angels play Bach for worship, but *en famille*, Mozart. Barth saw music as part of creation, performed and composed by humans, yet pointing to the divine creator behind it all. Music and text can witness to God in this way, and sometimes together. The idea was taken further by Dietrich Bonhoeffer. An excellent pianist, his writings are peppered with musical references which reveal a deep understanding of the machinery and power of music. His inner musical mind was sufficiently tuned that he could remember, 'hear' and reflect upon Bach's *Mass in B Minor* while in prison and having no access to any form of recording or score.

Bonhoeffer described life as 'polyphonic', and this was a comfort to him in the loneliness of imprisonment. Polyphony is music that has 'many sounds', in contrast to monody, a singular musical line. It is summed up in the difference between plainsong and Bach, between a soloist and a choir, between a worship song and a choral anthem. The harmonic base on which the music is built is called the *cantus firmus*. For Bonhoeffer, just as polyphonic music often involves a *cantus firmus*, so there are other melodies of life swirling above the ground bass of our being, which itself must be firm and secure. Human relationships can be viewed as life melodies which may soar and interact with the bass of faith in such a way that both are beautified and enhanced. As Christians, the life of faith is multidimensional and polyphonic.

Father God, you have blessed humanity with the gift of music with which to praise and glorify your creative and redeeming power revealed in Jesus Christ. By your Spirit, help us to sing with our souls inwardly and our voices outwardly that you may be praised worldwide, always. Amen

15 Benches

This was very displeasing to Jonah, and he became angry. He prayed to the Lord and said, 'O Lord! Is not this what I said while I was still in my own country? That is why I fled to Tarshish at the beginning; for I knew that you are a gracious God and merciful, slow to anger, and abounding in steadfast love, and ready to relent from punishing. And now, O Lord, please take my life from me, for it is better for me to die than to live.' And the Lord said, 'Is it right for you to be angry?' Then Jonah went out of the city and sat down east of the city, and made a booth for himself there. He sat under it in the shade, waiting to see what would become of the city.

The Lord God appointed a bush, and made it come up over Jonah, to give shade over his head, to save him from his discomfort; so Jonah was very happy about the bush. But when dawn came up the next day, God appointed a worm that attacked the bush, so that it withered. When the sun rose, God prepared a sultry east wind, and the sun beat down on the head of Jonah so that he was faint and asked that he might die. He said, 'It is better for me to die than to live.'

But God said to Jonah, 'Is it right for you to be angry about the bush?' And he said, 'Yes, angry enough to die.' Then the Lord said, 'You are concerned about the bush, for which you did not labour and which you did not grow; it came into being in a night and perished in a night. And should I not be concerned about Nineveh, that great city, in which there are more than a hundred and twenty thousand people who do not know their right hand from their left, and also many animals?'

JONAH 4

Near Rochester Cathedral is the King's Orchard, an ancient green space, which recently received a consignment of benches. These benches came from a national rose garden which had been forced to close to the public due to the pandemic. Many of the benches, which are now dispersed around the site, mostly underneath trees, commemorate people who died during the 20th century. These benches found a new home and new people to sit on them. This is perhaps sad to contemplate, but also rather lovely. In accepting these benches, we received more than wooden seats, for each one tells a story, and has been invested with loving memory.

Very often we find such benches in parks, beauty spots and other public areas, offering opportunity for rest, reflection or recuperation. To sit on a bench and admire the view is a simple pleasure. During the coronavirus pandemic, park benches were 'closed' with tape and signage, as were half the sinks in public lavatories and seats on trains. Social distancing denied many the opportunity to sit and reflect on the state of the world: to grieve, to pray, to admire the view. Now we can return to such simple habits and pleasures, we may forget this, but should avoid taking them for granted.

The reflective life is important. Rochester Cathedral is a Benedictine Foundation, which means that we read daily from the Rule of St Benedict at Morning Prayer. Benedict was born around 480 and died around 547. Each day a passage from the book he wrote to order the lifestyle of monasteries is read out loud, and it is at least interesting, and sometimes inspiring, to revisit the world of the sixth century and reflect on how much we have in common. Benedict's Rule is all about how to live in faithful Christian, hospitable community, which means it has something to say to us all about how we live together in global and local communities as well as religious ones. Human beings have not changed much, nor have the challenges and issues we face. Jesus knew this too, which is why so much of the sermon on the mount and his teachings on ethics have been transmitted so successfully and relevantly to our diverse and disparate world. Benedict's ancient translating of these 'tools' of life and faith of are as relevant now as they ever were.

Jonah's human nature is no different to ours, and he exhibits behaviour we can easily relate to. He was given a job he did not like or want and ultimately resents: to warn the people of Nineveh that they are sinners and to repent because trouble is coming. When God decides to spare the Ninevites from destruction, Jonah sulks. He sits down on the Old Testament equivalent of a bench under a tree, which he takes for granted, and sulks. Jonah resented God's forgiveness shown to others. He thinks and behaves like a disgruntled child. 'It's not fair', he says, as he folds his arms and plonks himself down by a bush. But this is not what benches or bushes are for. While many of us may have stomped off at times to stew on a bench, they are not intended as somewhere to park resentment, but rather to appreciate the generosity and mercy of God.

In life, both in general and in recent years, there is much to celebrate, but also much to resent if one is minded to. Many people resented Covid-19 restrictions, which while intended to save lives, still provoked anger, disobedience and childish reactions in some. These reactions can affect well-being. Jonah made his situation worse by sulking about a bush; his attitude caused him harm rather than good. Sometimes the way we react to events or conversations does us no good. Reflecting on our behaviour in serenity can help, and we sometimes need a reality check, just as God gave Jonah a reality check by means of the bush that came and went.

Benches are not always comfortable, especially for long periods: they are not generally for extended use. Similarly, time on a bench alone can cause spiritual discomfort. To be alone with one's thoughts can be refreshing, but not always for everyone. Dwelling on thoughts can be disconcerting, as some people do not like their own company, preferring the mental activity of chatter, conversation or gossip. Yet a little contemplative time and space can be beneficial to everyone, and anyone can acquire a taste for it.

We do not have to be spiritual giants to both learn and practise the quiet art of sitting on a bench in the beauty spot of the soul.

For many, the pandemic lockdowns were a deprivation of activity, sociability and even freedoms. Others found some benefit in the solitude the lockdowns imposed upon us – even if that solitude was enforced and lengthy, it may yet have sown the seeds of a reflective attitude which we may be able to continue to draw upon. If so, it can be seen as a silver lining to the dark cloud of Covid-19 which overshadowed not only our outdoor and indoor spaces, but our interior spaces too. So, as we enjoy the great outdoors, visiting public places and natural viewpoints where benches have been placed for our physical, spiritual and mental benefit, let us also spend some time on the interior.

Father God, who loves us in all our moods and feelings, be with us in all our contemplations and our busyness. When cast down by the cares of the world, may our spirits be lifted to you, and being so we may ever rejoice in your eternal mercy. Amen

16 Castles

[David] said:

The Lord is my rock, my fortress, and my deliverer,
   my God, my rock, in whom I take refuge,
my shield and the horn of my salvation,
   my stronghold and my refuge,
   my saviour; you save me from violence.
I call upon the Lord, who is worthy to be praised,
   and I am saved from my enemies.

For the waves of death encompassed me,
   the torrents of perdition assailed me;
the cords of Sheol entangled me,
   the snares of death confronted me.

In my distress I called upon the Lord;
   to my God I called.
From his temple he heard my voice,
   and my cry came to his ears…

For this I will extol you, O Lord, among the nations,
   and sing praises to your name.
He is a tower of salvation for his king,
   and shows steadfast love to his anointed,
   to David and his descendants forever.

2 SAMUEL 22:2–7, 50–51

Castles have two basic functions: to keep intruders out and to keep prisoners in. Some English castles have done both: Lancaster Castle and the Tower of London have been both strongholds and prisons in their time. Some castles have become schools, such as Atlantic College, based in St Donat's Castle in south Wales, where I went to school. In general, a castle is a structure built to protect those who dwell therein, and much romantic and historical drama speaks of the besieging of castles, or the liberation of captured prisoners. The romantic view is not always accurate – many castles are now ruins, and owning one and keeping it habitable and useable is a costly business. Many are tourist destinations, and as such reveal insights into various epochs and cultures. After 18 months of closure to the public in 2020–21, we can now visit castles once more and clamber among their ancient stones and gateways.

Castles are also places of the imagination: from Harry Potter's Hogwarts to Dracula's Castle, we can project our minds to a fictional world that never ceases to appeal. Castles are often the setting for labyrinthine computer games, with dark and dingy secret passageways concealing treasures or enemies, all rendered in virtual 3D. Castles can be mental spaces too, and there is a great biblical tradition of characterising God as a fortress or stronghold, in whom to reside and confide and shut out the assaults of enemies both spiritual and physical. Martin Luther's setting of Psalm 46, '*Ein feste Burg ist unser Gott*' ('A mighty fortress is our God') is a classic example, and here in 2 Samuel we hear David's voice of relief after his deliverance from Saul. Physical castles may rise and fall, but God is the only sure stronghold in which to hide and place our trust. Castles signify strength, project power and represent refuge, all sturdy metaphors of protection.

Castles also have many rooms, and it was this aspect that inspired Teresa of Ávila, the Spanish Carmelite nun, to compose her great spiritual work *The Interior Castle*, or *The Mansions* (*El Castillo Interior* or *Las Moradas*) in 1577. She had a vision of the human soul as a castle-shaped diamond, with seven interior chambers, each representing a stage of the journey through life. Advancement on this journey through the interior castle is by prayer in response to God's grace, humility and an exemplary life, which is not only defined by, but also expresses itself in, an aversion to sin. Progression deeper into the castle of the soul is made through union with God in prayer and meditation, and it becomes mystical, matrimonial even, as the journeying soul becomes wedded to Christ. Ultimately, in the seventh mansion the soul achieves clarity in prayer and a spiritual marriage with God. It is one of the great spiritual literary classics.

Such quasi-ecstatic, psychologically demanding and intense experiences of prayer and union with God do not inspire everyone, and the use of the word 'castle' can remind us of the impenetrability of God's divine nature. Yet Teresa gives us a glimpse of that secure interior stronghold of prayer and supplication, of which we may be reminded whenever we encounter a castle on our travels. Living in Rochester as I do, I am blessed with a Norman castle on my doorstep, opposite the cathedral. Constructed by Bishop Gundulf in 1089, it can represent God's faithfulness down the ages, but combined with David's words, I am also reminded of the strength of God's protection during times when the enemy attacked. Soon after the sealing of Magna Carta in 1215, King John besieged Rochester Castle, held by rebel barons with around a hundred knights, prevailing after two months. Castles fall eventually, but the stronghold of God is safe, says David.

In 2020–21 the world was besieged by Covid. Banished to the castles of our own homes, the doors were barred to visitors and intruders, and the battle was to keep the virus out, brought in as it so easily could be by friends, family and strangers alike. Behind the barricades of our own front doors, we tried to stay safe and stay at home. Waves of death encompassed the nation, and in distress many called upon the Lord. For some the prayers from lockdown castles were answered by good neighbourly behaviour, compliance with guidelines and vaccinations. Others saw the ensuing battle as a scientific campaign of technology against mutating nature and would not attribute any aspect of the pandemic's chaos to any divine cause or intervention.

Ultimately, some people see the hand of God in human endeavour, healing and flourishing, while others do not or refuse to. We all know what happened over that period, and the great extent to which human skill and knowledge contributed to the alleviation of suffering and the release from the confinements of our homes. However we interpret it, we can remember David and his praise and thanksgiving for rescue and release, whose voice was heard and whose cries came to God, who ultimately delivered him, and delivers us, from invasions of body and soul.

Next time you visit or see an ancient castle, silhouetted against the sky perhaps, remember how your home became a castle, and remember all those who fell in the coronavirus siege and those who now rest secure in God in that eternal stronghold of everlasting life, won for us through the death and resurrection of Jesus Christ our Lord.

O God our strength and fortress, we thank you for your protection and care. Be merciful to those who are besieged by the assaults of life, that in you they may find hope, faith and love. Amen

17 **Haircuts**

[Delilah] said to [Samson], 'How can you say, "I love you", when your heart is not with me? You have mocked me three times now and have not told me what makes your strength so great.' Finally, after she had nagged him with her words day after day, and pestered him, he was tired to death. So he told her his whole secret, and said to her, 'A razor has never come upon my head; for I have been a nazirite to God from my mother's womb. If my head were shaved, then my strength would leave me; I would become weak, and be like anyone else.'

When Delilah realised that he had told her his whole secret, she sent and called the lords of the Philistines, saying, 'This time come up, for he has told his whole secret to me.' Then the lords of the Philistines came up to her, and brought the money in their hands. She let him fall asleep on her lap; and she called a man, and had him shave off the seven locks of his head. He began to weaken, and his strength left him. Then she said, 'The Philistines are upon you, Samson!' When he awoke from his sleep, he thought, 'I will go out as at other times, and shake myself free.' But he did not know that the Lord had left him. So the Philistines seized him and gouged out his eyes. They brought him down to Gaza and bound him with bronze shackles; and he ground at the mill in the prison. But the hair of his head began to grow again after it had been shaved.

JUDGES 16:15–22

One of the privations of the Covid lockdowns was the inability to have a haircut. Although life was put on hold, hair kept growing! For many, haircare is not simply about appearance and tidiness, but

about self-care and well-being. Seeing friends, or being seen, even on Zoom, with unkempt hair became for some people an embarrassment. The whole nation had become dishevelled by Covid-19.

All mammals have hair, fine protein filaments, emerging from the skin. The only living part of hair is the follicle, from which the hair grows, which lies below the skin. Although Jesus told his disciples that 'even the hairs of your head are all counted' (Matthew 10:30), hair colour affects how many strands are on your head. Blonde people tend to have the most, with around 150,000 follicles at birth. Brown-haired people have about 110,000. The majority of the world is black-haired, with 100,000 hairs. A mere 2% of humans are redheads, and these have around 90,000 hair follicles. But the hair on your head represents a small proportion: the entire body has around 5 million hair follicles. Even though we may think of ourselves as basically hairless creatures, we have hair almost everywhere. It is there for a reason: warmth, protection and to alert us to movement.

Nowadays hair is considered a thing of beauty, on which to lavish attention, money and effort, whether in shaving, trimming, shaping or even extending it. The way we, or others treat our hair, can reflect attitudes, beliefs or status. The Roundheads, who fought against Charles I in the English Civil War, were so called because of their sparse haircuts (in contrast to regal ringlets), and the idea that a particular hairstyle reflects allegiance to a group has remained to the present day. Hairstyles come and go. In more modern times, shaved heads have taken on new meanings – concentration-camp prisoners' heads were shaved; soldiers often have crew cuts; and a shaved head can be a symptom of various cancer treatments. Our hairstyle can have meaning, which can be 'read', interpreted, judged.

Hairstyles also have religious significance. Micah says: 'Make yourselves bald and cut off your hair for your pampered children; make yourselves as bald as the eagle, for they have gone from you into exile' (Micah 1:16). In the Jewish law, shaving as a sign of mourning (a pagan practice) was forbidden (Deuteronomy 14:1), although the

Egyptians shaved regularly and allowed their hair to grow as a sign of mourning. Ezekiel is clear on priestly haircare: 'They shall not shave their heads or let their locks grow long; they shall only trim the hair of their heads' (Ezekiel 44:20). The traditional idea that women grow their hair longer than men finds its origin in Hebrew culture, imported into Christianity by the apostle Paul, who attempted to be uncontentious by devoting a bit of 1 Corinthians to the subject: 'If a man wears long hair, it is degrading to him, but if a woman has long hair, it is her glory' (1 Corinthians 11:14–15). Other faiths have various teachings and practices concerning hair and beards, most of which relate to decency, status, devotion or discipline, particularly Sikhism, Islam and Buddhism. Any discussion about hair among religions highlights differences, discrepancies and sometimes disputes.

Which brings us to Samson. The vows of Nazirites are found in Numbers 6 and include abstentions from drinking wine, cutting their hair or going near the dead. Indeed the only occasion when they must shave their head is if they find themselves in the proximity of death. This means that when Samson succumbs to Delilah's pleading as to the cause of his strength, he is not only showing an emotional weakness that will cause physical weakness, he is committing a sin. There is also a resonance of him being in the proximity of his own death. He had vowed not to shave his head, but by revealing his secret he effectively permits it. His haircut is a power cut too: a punishment for breaking his vow, and so the Lord 'leaves him', only to return as Samson's locks naturally return. The bald moral of the tale is that if you desert God, God will desert you. Without God, Samson is exposed and powerless.

In Christ it is not so, for 'God is faithful, and he will not let you be tested beyond your strength, but with the testing he will also provide the way out so that you may be able to endure it' (1 Corinthians 10:13). Samson was tested beyond his strength, but in Christ we have a stronger bond, a tie of loyalty that is located in the ultimate rescue, redemption, restoration and renewal that comes through his cross and resurrection. Samson succumbed to the temptation to reject God, whereas Jesus did not (Matthew 4:1–11), and it is therefore Jesus, not Samson, in whom we find inspiration. Whatever follicular foibles we have that determine what we do with our hair, we have power in Christ to withstand that which weakens, humiliates, damages or even destroys us.

God, who has numbered the hairs of our head, care for us in our weakness, that in faith and hope we made be strong in the knowledge of your love and grow in grace all the days of our life. Amen

18 **Furlough**

'For the kingdom of heaven is like a landowner who went out early in the morning to hire labourers for his vineyard. After agreeing with the labourers for the usual daily wage, he sent them into his vineyard. When he went out about nine o'clock, he saw others standing idle in the marketplace; and he said to them, "You also go into the vineyard, and I will pay you whatever is right." So they went. When he went out again about noon and about three o'clock, he did the same. And about five o'clock he went out and found others standing around; and he said to them, "Why are you standing here idle all day?" They said to him, "Because no one has hired us." He said to them, "You also go into the vineyard." When evening came, the owner of the vineyard said to his manager, "Call the labourers and give them their pay, beginning with the last and then going to the first." When those hired about five o'clock came, each of them received the usual daily wage. Now when the first came, they thought they would receive more; but each of them also received the usual daily wage. And when they received it, they grumbled against the landowner, saying, "These last worked only one hour, and you have made them equal to us who have borne the burden of the day and the scorching heat." But he replied to one of them, "Friend, I am doing you no wrong; did you not agree with me for the usual daily wage? Take what belongs to you and go; I choose to give to this last the same as I give to you. Am I not allowed to do what I choose with what belongs to me? Or are you envious because I am generous?" So the last will be first, and the first will be last.'

MATTHEW 20:1–16

By the end of 2020 around 9.6 million jobs, from 1.2 million different employers, had been furloughed in the UK as part of the government's pandemic job-retention scheme. The scheme was introduced to protect jobs and subsidise employers who continued to employ staff even though it was not physically possible or safe for them to turn up to work because of Covid-19. About half of the population of the UK have jobs – in 2019 the figure was 32.7 million, which means that nearly a third of the workforce were furloughed in 2020, if only for a short while. This was a turning upside down of the norm: people were paid not to work; indeed, under the scheme they were not allowed to.

The word 'furlough' has several original uses, deriving initially from a 17th-century Dutch word meaning 'leave of absence', and it is used by the military and in the Christian missionary field. For a missionary, a furlough is when they return home from their labours in the Christian vineyard abroad, to be with their families and to relax, rest and recharge their spiritual batteries. It is a kind of an extended sabbath.

This brings us to the parable of furlough: the story told by Jesus about first-century vineyard workers. Both annoying and delightful to his hearers and to us, it reveals that God's ways are not our ways. God turns upside down the idea that people should be paid by the hour rather than what they need to live. In a world where the first shall be first and the last must fend for themselves, Jesus says that is not God's way, that is not what the kingdom of heaven is like. The kingdom of heaven is more like a place where people get paid even if they have laboured little. It is a bit like a place where a third of the workforce are on furlough through no fault of their own. For a loaf of bread costs the same to everyone, rich and poor alike, and everyone needs to and has a right to eat.

It is so obvious to us that an hourly wage is fair, such that someone who works ten hours in the heat should be paid ten times more than someone who works only one. It is so obvious in fact that it really is worth examining or questioning. For when we do so, we realise that the rules of the vineyard – the rules of Christian living – are different.

We cannot do anything to earn a place in the kingdom of God. Rather, we accept what a generous God gives us as grace. The rules of the vineyard are made by the God and Father of all, whose mode of being is about generosity, not rights, and from whom life is a gift, and for whom justice is loving mercy.

We saw the outworking of this when, during the lockdown of March 2020, many saw their Christian mission as consisting of feeding the hungry, in all sorts of creative and modern ways, from food banks to cooking meals and leaving food on doorsteps. It was a generosity that transcended pecking orders and self-centredness and enabled many to exercise Christian principles in response to a national crisis. And some of these people did not profess to be Christians at all.

In that sense, the crisis was an opportunity for those who had an inner passion for service, an inner love for their neighbours, and an inner desire to live out the gospel message of equality, release, faith, hope and love. Many of those people I worked with in north London at that time were on furlough, and so in one sense their predicament released them to help. The government were effectively paying them to do it. But they didn't *have* to do it, so to join in was genuinely an act of service, care and compassion.

It was a joy to behold, enable and participate in. As I filled the boot of my car with loaves of bread, arranged for a youth hostel's food stocks to be distributed to a children's home, and scurried to and fro on empty roads in response to requests on the WhatsApp coronavirus group (which had members from all faith communities), there was a frisson, a buzz and a sense of not only being able to help, but being able to do something that made a difference and, equally important, of doing it *together*. As a Christian, there was something 'first century' about it. We had gone back to basics: feeding the hungry, consoling the sick, looking out for the weak, and sharing out what there was and what was given (Acts 4:32–35).

This all happened not very long ago, and we should never forget it. The pandemic was a terrible thing, but in the midst of it came upside-down action inspired by faith, hope and love.

God of work and play, joy and sorrow, justice and love, have pity on all who cannot find work, who have lost their jobs or whose jobs are demeaning, distressing or oppressive. Give us all grace to serve one another in authentically Christian ways, inspired always by the example and teaching of your Son, our Saviour Jesus Christ. Amen

19 Alcoholic drinks

Do not try to prove your strength by wine-drinking,
    for wine has destroyed many.
As the furnace tests the work of the smith,
    so wine tests hearts when the insolent quarrel.
Wine is very life to human beings
    if taken in moderation.
What is life to one who is without wine?
    It has been created to make people happy.
Wine drunk at the proper time and in moderation
    is rejoicing of heart and gladness of soul.
Wine drunk to excess leads to bitterness of spirit,
    to quarrels and stumbling.
Drunkenness increases the anger of a fool to his own hurt,
    reducing his strength and adding wounds.
Do not reprove your neighbour at a banquet of wine,
    and do not despise him in his merrymaking;
speak no word of reproach to him,
    and do not distress him by making demands of him.

SIRACH (ECCLESIASTICUS) 31:25–31

During the pandemic lockdowns, the hospitality industry, which includes pubs and restaurants, closed for extended periods. Beer was poured down drains, and some distilleries focused on manufacturing hand gel because it often contains alcohol. The consumption of beer, wine and spirits took place almost exclusively at home at this time, and shops and supermarkets sold an extra 12.6 million litres of alcohol in 2020–21 than the previous year (a 24.4% increase). In one survey, 58.6% of people reported drinking more, and research by Public

Health England showed that lockdowns affected heavy drinkers the most. If the Covid-19 pandemic resulted in a long-term increase in drinking, the prognosis looks bleak. Liver disease is already the second leading cause of premature death in people of working age. Alcoholism is a serious issue in so many societies and is destructive not only for the drinker, but also for relationships and loved ones who are often its unseen victims.

Alcoholic drinks, like many aspects of life that can harm us, are not morally good or bad in themselves. Moderation in all things is a useful maxim, and as such, a drink of wine, beer or gin and tonic can be relaxing, refreshing and socially cohesive to those who are not suffering or recovering from alcoholism. Churches have made alcoholic drinks over the centuries, such as Benedictine, Dom Pérignon champagne and Trappist beers, and more recently a handful of cathedrals have marketed their own gins – although some say that gin, known as 'mother's ruin' because of its vast consumption in the 18th century, is not something that Mother Church should be pedalling, even in a good cause.

Indeed, drinking alcohol has divided opinion for millennia. Proverbs acknowledges the dangers of being led astray by drink: 'Wine is a mocker, strong drink a brawler, and whoever is led astray by it is not wise' (Proverbs 20:1); 'It is not for kings to drink wine, or for rulers to desire strong drink; or else they will drink and forget what has been decreed, and will pervert the rights of all the afflicted' (Proverbs 31:4–5). Paul also cautioned his readers against drunkenness: 'Do not get drunk with wine, for that is debauchery; but be filled with the Spirit' (Ephesians 5:18). Yet to say that the Bible forbids, or even frowns on, drinking alcohol is a mistake. There is much wine-drinking in the Bible, including many occasions when Jesus and his disciples drink wine (most notably, the wedding at Cana and the last supper). As a staple liquid of the day, it features in many parables and metaphors – the good Samaritan, for example, pours wine on the wounds of the traveller who is robbed on the road (Luke 10:34). The French reformer John Calvin claimed that 'wine is God's special drink.

The purpose of good wine is to inspire us to a livelier sense of gratitude to God.'

Biblical authors knew about wine from experience and observation, and the way in which we find wisdom, caution and acceptance of alcohol in the Bible reveals that the social problems associated with overindulgence were similar to those of today.

These range of attitudes towards wine that we see in the Bible can also be extended to the consumption of other alcoholic drinks. Just as wine was a safe alternative to water in the ancient Near East (the water was often dirty and known to carry disease), beer occupied a similar status in more northern climes, where barley and hops grow. Known to impair the faculties if overindulged, beer was relied on as a safe drink for people of all ages, to an extent that might surprise us. At the beginning of the 19th century, when Maria Hackett discovered that the St Paul's Cathedral choristers were being paid in beer for singing in theatres, she campaigned for better conditions for them.

Meanwhile 1,300 years earlier, Benedict wrote in his Rule:

> It is with some misgiving we appoint the measure of other men's living: however, duly considering the infirmity of the weak we believe that half a pint of wine per head per day suffices; but let those to whom God gives the power of the endurance of abstinence know that they shall have their due reward.

Yet, acknowledging the tradition of the Nazirite who is set apart for not touching alcohol (see Numbers 6:1–5), Benedict also wrote:

> Although we read that wine is by no means for monks, yet because in our time monks cannot be persuaded to see this, at all events let us agree as to this, that we will not drink to satiety, but somewhat sparingly, because: 'Wine makes even the wise to fall away.'

Most of us are not monks or Nazirites, and none of us live in the first, sixth or 19th centuries. Temperance movements have come and gone, and Mormons and Muslims do not drink alcohol at all. Such a position is worthy of respect, but whether it is morally or spiritually superior is not obvious to Christians whose Messiah drank wine both socially and symbolically. The Eucharist, after all, employs bread and wine, the basic food and drink of Jesus' day. For the Christian, we give thanks in all things but also exercise moderation likewise.

God our creator, we thank you who gave us the fruits of the earth to gladden the heart and sustain us in need. Help us always to respect your bounty, to act with moderation and self-respect and to care for the weak and distressed. Pour out your mercy on those who are bowed down by addiction or lack of self-control, that all your children may find joy and pleasure in your good gifts and companionship of true fellowship in Jesus Christ our Lord. Amen

20 Fruit

Then Jesus said to the crowds and to his disciples, 'The scribes and the Pharisees sit on Moses' seat; therefore, do whatever they teach you and follow it; but do not do as they do, for they do not practise what they teach. They tie up heavy burdens, hard to bear, and lay them on the shoulders of others; but they themselves are unwilling to lift a finger to move them. They do all their deeds to be seen by others; for they make their phylacteries broad and their fringes long...

'Woe to you, scribes and Pharisees, hypocrites! For you tithe mint, dill, and cummin, and have neglected the weightier matters of the law: justice and mercy and faith. It is these you ought to have practised without neglecting the others. You blind guides! You strain out a gnat but swallow a camel!

'Woe to you, scribes and Pharisees, hypocrites! For you clean the outside of the cup and of the plate, but inside they are full of greed and self-indulgence. You blind Pharisee! First clean the inside of the cup, so that the outside also may become clean.

'Woe to you, scribes and Pharisees, hypocrites! For you are like whitewashed tombs, which on the outside look beautiful, but inside they are full of the bones of the dead and of all kinds of filth. So you also on the outside look righteous to others, but inside you are full of hypocrisy and lawlessness.'

MATTHEW 23:1–5, 23–28

Near Rochester Cathedral is the King's Orchard, a haven of peace and beauty, with beehives, cherry trees and flowers, wonderfully kept. It is reputedly where King Henry VIII met Anne of Cleves on New Year's

Day 1540. It was not a happy meeting, for when the king tried to woo Anne by dressing up, she did not recognise him, which did not amuse Henry. The union was doomed from the start – neither Henry nor Anne were what the other was expecting.

The King's Orchard is full of apple trees. Walking through the orchard in the late summer, there are apples ready to pick along with windfalls on the ground, which are good for making pies, crumbles, jams and sauces. Some are better than others, however, and you cannot always tell the good from the bad. A perfect-looking apple can be deceptive; all that glistens is not golden delicious. Inside, hidden from view, there may be unpleasantness lurking. As the old joke goes, what is worse than biting into an apple and finding a worm? Finding half a worm.

Conversely, an apple with blemishes, dents and dirt on the skin can yet be wonderfully tasty and eminently edible. Just add raisins and honey, and bake for half an hour!

When Jesus criticised the scribes and Pharisees, he was clear that the core of faith needs to be clean, even if the skin is dirty. Dirty skin does not mean a dirty heart, and vice versa, just as an apple can have blemishes on the skin but be perfectly all right, or an apple can be rotten to the core without revealing the fact on the outside. The inner and outer life are connected, but they can be distinguished, for they can contradict one another – and therein lies hypocrisy or turmoil.

We should not judge a book by its cover. The poet Chaucer wrote in the Canon's Yeoman's tale of *The Canterbury Tales*: 'But al thyng which that shyneth as the gold nis nat gold, as that I have herd it told.' Shakespeare said likewise in *The Merchant of Venice*, where the Prince of Morocco refers to Portia's puzzling, glittering box of delights:

All that glisters is not gold – often have you heard that told.
Many a man his life hath sold but my outside to behold.
Gilded tombs do worms enfold.
Act 2, scene 7

Things are not always what they seem, whether they be a rotten apple, a wolf in sheep's clothing, an advertising campaign or a political manifesto. Sometimes even our best friend can turn out to be despicable, and that rocks our world.

Likewise, a coronavirus can lurk in someone who shows no symptoms, making it, and them, an unseen danger. It is not their fault, but what can come from within can damage them and others. The responsibilities we had to learn towards ourselves and others in relation to Covid testing, isolation, vaccinations, mask-wearing and human interaction all have their spiritual parallel. For, as Jesus might have said, hypocrisy is a virus: it is hidden within, it mutates and it is dangerously infectious. We need to be inoculated against it, as washing one's hands is not sufficient.

Handwashing is a physical precaution against a physical phenomenon, yet the Pharisees believed that handwashing solved spiritual uncleanliness (see Mark 7:1–5). Covid-19 taught us that this is not so: it is only part of the picture and an integrated approach is necessary, one that encompasses outward cleanliness, inner inoculation, outward expression of care for others and an inner serenity that 'accepts the things I cannot change, has courage to change the things I can and wisdom to know the difference', as Reinhold Niebuhr (1892–1971) said.

As we endeavour to learn from the pandemic years, we might remember that what is unseen can be deceptive and dangerous, and what lies underneath is not always very savoury, in ourselves or others. This is true physically and spiritually. So, rather than judge others, we hold our own inner cleanliness before God, seeking forgiveness and encouragement in faith, hope and love, assured always of his loving mercy and redeeming grace.

Creator God, who knows the core of our being and the secrets of our hearts, by your grace and mercy cleanse and heal our inner rottenness, that we may be released into renewed, resurrection life, opened up for us by your Son, Jesus Christ our Saviour. Amen

21 Rainbows

'And you, be fruitful and multiply, abound on the earth and multiply in it.'

Then God said to Noah and to his sons with him, 'As for me, I am establishing my covenant with you and your descendants after you, and with every living creature that is with you, the birds, the domestic animals, and every animal of the earth with you, as many as came out of the ark. I establish my covenant with you, that never again shall all flesh be cut off by the waters of a flood, and never again shall there be a flood to destroy the earth.' God said, 'This is the sign of the covenant that I make between me and you and every living creature that is with you, for all future generations: I have set my bow in the clouds, and it shall be a sign of the covenant between me and the earth. When I bring clouds over the earth and the bow is seen in the clouds, I will remember my covenant that is between me and you and every living creature of all flesh; and the waters shall never again become a flood to destroy all flesh. When the bow is in the clouds, I will see it and remember the everlasting covenant between God and every living creature of all flesh that is on the earth.' God said to Noah, 'This is the sign of the covenant that I have established between me and all flesh that is on the earth.'

GENESIS 9:7–17

Did you join the new religion during the pandemic? I am not referring to online worship, streaming services, virtual choirs and orchestras, and WhatsApp groups. That was the old religion done anew. There was also a new form of 'church' that arose, involving a secular ritual.

During spring and early summer 2020 at 8.00 pm every Thursday, millions of people applauded NHS staff and key workers who took risks and served us sacrificially. You may recall the heart-breaking stories of those who died in the line of duty, young and old. So, galvanised by a woman from Holland who got people clapping, we boldly stepped outside to offer praise and thanksgiving to these marvellous people. All this applauding was both audible and laudable. In no small way, it also made people feel a bit better about the situation we all found ourselves in. It was at least *something* we could all do, if we wished.

The public clapping was quite close to the concept of worship, which means to offer honour to a worthy object or person. For several months, we in a sense worshipped the NHS. Our doctors and nurses became the priests and deacons of physical ministry. It became a new weekly ritual with new unity and new purpose, built on a blend of appreciation and fear. These are archetypal religious motivations that direct our hopes and prayers skywards, from where the rainbow – the logo of that new worship – sends its beams upon us.

This rainbow motif has its origins in the biblical flood story. Even those who do not comprehend its cultural heritage or original meaning still recognise the rainbow as a sign of hope. It has taken on meaning as a symbol of solidarity in other contexts, too, and another aspect of the NHS rainbow is the sense of 'standing alongside' the key workers. The idea of worship blends this spectrum of emotional colours.

A rainbow is etched into the canvas of the great novel of that name by D.H. Lawrence – an all-encompassing arc over family relationships. Published in 1915, *The Rainbow* tells the story of three generations of the Brangwen family. As we travel the wide arc of their family history, we encounter a profound exposition of passion and power amid the familiar social roles of husbands, wives, children and parents. We meet Ursula Brangwen, whose ongoing exploits are continued with that of her sister Gudrun in the sequel, *Women in Love*. She sees 'in the rainbow the earth's new architecture, the old, brittle corruption of houses and factories swept away, the world built up in a living fabric of Truth, fitting to the over-arching heaven'. It is to be the optimistic dawn of a new modernist age, in which the idea of truth is to be recast. World War I – the war of machines – had begun, but it is the ancient, religious, biblical, hopeful symbol of the rainbow that Lawrence uses to span the arcs of his magisterial literature. For Lawrence, the archetypal themes of flood and covenant are transformed into an ebb and flow of passion ameliorated by power, and as the book concludes the catalogue of trials and tribulations of young lives confused and conflicted by passion, they are given a hopeful future in the rainbow which recolours and brightens life.

Whether it is Lawrence's metaphorical rainbows arching over a world ripped by war and ravaged by Spanish flu, or the children's drawings we saw in front windows, we are so much reminded of the power and promise of the rainbow in what was and remains our current, damaged, challenging age. For many, the rainbow became the badge of the modern cult of clapping for key workers, offered from a nation locked down in the arks of their homes, floating on a flood of fear that brought isolation, tension and lamentable loss as many went overboard and were lost to the waves of Covid-19.

The 2007 film *Evan Almighty* is a contemporary recasting of the story of Noah's ark, set in the USA. Fantastical, and arguably trivial in some senses, the film nevertheless has a recurring theme, which is that the world can be changed through Acts of Random Kindness, or ARK. Now the 'rain' of the virus has stopped pouring down upon us so relentlessly, we are still navigating the waters which bear us away from a traumatic few years. We still need many ARKs, as we always have done, in fact. So let us strive to be kind in all sorts of both random and targeted ways, praying always for those for whom the waters are stormy and the pandemic a soul-destroying memory.

And through it all, let us always remember to offer praise and thanking for those who serve others, yet while worshipping only the God and Father of our Lord Jesus Christ.

O God of earth, sea and sky, you guided Noah through the floods of isolation and continue to inspire your people to help others. We thank you for all who minister to our faith, well-being and health, and ask for your grace to recognise your hand of hope in the whole of creation. Amen

22 The moon

It is the moon that marks the changing seasons,
   governing the times, their everlasting sign.
From the moon comes the sign for festal days,
   a light that wanes when it completes its course.
The new moon, as its name suggests, renews itself;
   how marvellous it is in this change,
a beacon to the hosts on high,
   shining in the vault of the heavens!

SIRACH (ECCLESIASTICUS) 43:6–8

Just before the pandemic struck and lockdowns were declared in the UK, Rochester Cathedral hosted a large replica of the moon. Filled with gas and suspended from the nave roof, it attracted 120,000 visitors in a month. Designed by the artist Luke Jerram, the moon installation was a fusion of lunar imagery, moonlight and surround sound composition. It has travelled the world and been hosted by many cathedrals and large sites, usually free to the public. At London's Natural History Museum, 2.1 million people saw it in six months.

So many people came to see it in Rochester that cathedral administrative staff abandoned their 'day jobs' to act as crowd managers, welcomers and hosts, along with many volunteers. It was a huge success in inviting local people into the building, many of whom had never been before. There were also moon-themed concerts, acts of worship, children's activities and a romantic evening under the moon, at which couples were given a rose and a glass of fizz. (One pair got engaged under this inflatable moon of love.)

A few weeks later, the cathedral, along with other places of worship and heritage sites, was completely closed, a sad consequence of an increasingly powerful pandemic. Luke Jerram contracted Covid in November 2020 and has since made sculptures of not only the virus itself but also the AstraZeneca vaccine. He has also made models of Mars and Gaia (earth).

What on earth inspired so many, of all ages and backgrounds, to come and see a replica moon? After all, it is visible, at least in part, on most clear nights of the year and always has been. Fascinating as the moon has been to every culture and generation, it is hardly mentioned in the New Testament. This is likely because of the range of religious deities throughout the Middle East (and worldwide) which are lunar. It is no surprise that thousands of years ago the moon should be personified and worshipped, not least because of its influence on tides, weather patterns and even human cycles. Many calendars were set by the phases of the moon, which were reliable and regular. The Greek goddesses Selene and Artemis (worshipped in Ephesus) and the Roman goddess Luna would have been familiar to Jesus' generation.

Everyone on earth – Jesus and his disciples among them – has looked at the same moon. And eventually, in 1969, humans walked on its surface. The effects of the moon landing are still to be felt perhaps, and subsequent explorations of space – with unmanned craft going as far as Pluto – have stretched our knowledge and imaginations. For some, these astronomical discoveries have challenged their faith in an earthbound creator God; for others, it has underlined the vastness of creation, the greatness of God and the uniqueness of our situation and context as sentient beings on a blue planet swirling in the midst of nothingness. We are no closer to answering the question 'Is there anybody out there?'; we just understand the question differently, and answer it with mathematical probabilities rather than any evidence, which we simply do not have the ability or lifespan to collect.

Since the first moon landing we now know far more about what we do not know. There is more room for God, not less. Apollo 11 astronaut

Buzz Aldrin revealed that he took Holy Communion to the moon and consumed it there. There is no place on earth, nor in the heavens, where God cannot go and be.

That is, of course, if you believe any of it happened at all. Some people did not, and to some extent still do not, believe the moon landing actually took place and that instead it was a stunt to impress the Soviets and assert American technological superiority; that it was carefully fabricated to be seen to meet President Kennedy's dream and pretend to 'win' a race that galvanised a fearful generation. Professor Brian Cox is sufficiently exercised by the preposterous idea that people do not believe it happened to post 'proofs' on the internet. The idea that it was a hoax is incredible.

We might connect the moon landing to the resurrection, and ask which is more believable, or unbelievable: that God should raise Jesus from the dead or that we should get human beings on and off the moon safely? If one is more 'believable' than the other, how and why is that? For one is an observable experience with eyewitnesses which is treated at least by some people as something which may or may not be believed. The other is an observable experience with eyewitnesses which is treated at least by some people as something which may or may not be believed.

What the moon landing teaches us is that, even if cameras, newsreels and documentaries had been available, such that the risen Christ could have been filmed and Mary Magdalene interviewed for *Newsnight*, there would still have been people who would not have believed it. We cannot demand the same means and standards of reporting truth we operate today of an event that happened so long ago, but we do have the standards of evidence they had so long ago. Eyewitness accounts have always been valid, however reported. And there are folk – billions of them past and present – who have believed in the death and resurrection of Jesus Christ.

We might remember this when we gaze heavenward on a cloudless night and see the ancient moon, placed perfectly in our skies, that the creating, redeeming, sustaining love of God transcends our beliefs, our thoughts and our world.

O Lord our Sovereign, how majestic is your name in all the earth! You have set your glory above the heavens, and when we look at the moon and the stars that you have established, we wonder that you are mindful of us mortals whom you create, love and sustain, now and always. Amen

23 Lakes

[Jesus] made the disciples get into the boat and go on ahead to the other side, while he dismissed the crowds. And after he had dismissed the crowds, he went up the mountain by himself to pray. When evening came, he was there alone, but by this time the boat, battered by the waves, was far from the land, for the wind was against them. And early in the morning he came walking towards them on the lake. But when the disciples saw him walking on the lake, they were terrified, saying, 'It is a ghost!' And they cried out in fear. But immediately Jesus spoke to them and said, 'Take heart, it is I; do not be afraid.'

Peter answered him, 'Lord, if it is you, command me to come to you on the water.' He said, 'Come.' So Peter got out of the boat, started walking on the water, and came towards Jesus. But when he noticed the strong wind, he became frightened, and beginning to sink, he cried out, 'Lord, save me!' Jesus immediately reached out his hand and caught him, saying to him, 'You of little faith, why did you doubt?' When they got into the boat, the wind ceased.

And those in the boat worshipped him, saying, 'Truly you are the Son of God.'

MATTHEW 14:22–33

A lake often conveys a great sense of calm, of still waters, reflecting the universe above, like a sheet of mirrored glass. A lake also conceals its depths. It might be only a few metres deep or its surface might cover unfathomable depths, like Loch Ness in Scotland, which at 230 metres is the second-deepest body of water in the UK, after Loch Morar.

Loch Ness holds more than a cubic mile of water, which is room for a lot of sunken boats, monsters and a deep imagination.

The surface of a lake holds a tension between the sky and the depths: a permeable barrier between the seen and the unseen. If we look directly into a lake we invariably see our own reflection, and if we look across a lake we see its shoreline refracted on its surface. The fact is, one cannot 'see' a lake, it is simply a body of transparent water which reveals what is around and above, but rarely below it.

The Sea of Galilee is actually a lake, known also as Lake Tiberias. It is the lowest freshwater lake in the world and is 64.4 square miles when full, with a maximum depth of approximately 43 metres. It is fed by underground springs, but mostly by the River Jordan. Like almost all lakes it is full of fresh water, rather than salty sea water. Jesus walked on it, calmed a storm on it, fished in it and had breakfast beside it. As such, it was for him and his disciples a place of calling, mystery, fear, work, leisure, serenity and, ultimately, post-resurrection reconciliation. It became a place of deep and lasting memories and, although the weather upon it is very changeable, it has hardly changed.

For this reason it is a powerful place of pilgrimage to this day, for its waters give as close a sense of the historical Jesus as any of the physically built sites in its ever-changing, politically influenced and in some cases militarily bombarded environs. The Galilean lake – the 'Syrian Sea' as the hymn writer John Whittier called it in the much-loved 'Dear Lord and Father of Mankind' (although he never intended it to be a hymn) – truly is a place where one might hear 'the gracious calling of the Lord' in the place where Jesus really knelt, and where 'the silence of eternity' may be felt in, beneath or above the waters that transcend the passage of time. On the surface of a lake, one can sense the pastness of the present and the presence of the past.

Lakes are also metaphors for the mind, and it is perhaps no coincidence that Whittier's hymn refers to the 'strain and stress' of life and asks prayerfully that we be 'reclothed in our rightful mind'. Most of us live – and are seen to live – on that fine surface of the water, the boundary between the turmoil of the skies and the hidden depths impenetrable to the human eye. In recent years, preceding the challenges of the pandemic, awareness of mental health issues has been increasing. Members of the royal family and other celebrities have made it okay to not be okay, and have spoken openly, bravely and honestly about submerged illnesses and conditions that have made sufferers feel judged, isolated or stigmatised. With the Covid-19 pandemic taking a widespread and evident toll on public mental health and well-being, it may even be said that increasing awareness, tolerance and understanding of mental health has been a positive outcome of the damage the pandemic did to national and individual psyches. There were human storms during the pandemic, but the ripples on the surface were noticed and the turmoil below recognised, to some extent. Many have walked on the surface of stormy lakes these past few years, and the thought that Jesus walked there too and calmed the storms can be a great comfort.

Whichever district our favourite lakes may be in, their peaceful beauty and the life they sustain in their fresh, deep and living waters can conceal a danger. The danger is a depth of despair and death into which one can so easily fall when storms above cloud our vision and disconnect faith, hope and love. So in the lakes of our lives, we hold a balance, between fear and love, between doubt and faith, and between despair and hope. The coronavirus pandemic gave us downpours of all six of these things, and now that that storm has abated it is time to live, and learn, and act, and pray.

Dear Lord and Father of humankind, give us rest by the lakes of our lives, that the strains and stresses of our troubled minds may be reclothed in your love, and that we may kneel with Jesus to share in eternal prayer till, summoned by your call, all our strivings cease. Amen

Autumn

24 The sea

On that day, when evening had come, he said to them, 'Let us go across to the other side.' And leaving the crowd behind, they took him with them in the boat, just as he was. Other boats were with him. A great gale arose, and the waves beat into the boat, so that the boat was already being swamped. But he was in the stern, asleep on the cushion; and they woke him up and said to him, 'Teacher, do you not care that we are perishing?' He woke up and rebuked the wind, and said to the sea, 'Peace! Be still!' Then the wind ceased, and there was a dead calm. He said to them, 'Why are you afraid? Have you still no faith?' And they were filled with great awe and said to one another, 'Who then is this, that even the wind and the sea obey him?'

MARK 4:35–41

As we saw in the previous chapter, the Sea of Galilee is not a sea, strictly speaking, but it does behave like one. Winds stir up strong waves and dangerous storms can arise – and dissipate – swiftly. For a local fisherman or sailor caught in such a storm, it made little difference whether they were on a freshwater lake or in the salty sea; they would respect the waters. To paraphrase Psalm 107:

Those who go down to the sea in ships, doing business on the mighty waters see the deeds of the Lord; his wondrous works in the deep. The waves of the sea raise them up to heaven, and

down to the depths; reeling and staggering in the swell until they cry to the Lord in distress, who makes the storm be still, and hushes the waves of the sea.

This psalm forms the background to this biblical story, and the disciples would have known it.

The sea is a vast primeval force, a highway for trade, a fish warehouse and a place of recreation but also a very dangerous place to be. It covers two-thirds of the earth's surface and its depths are far greater than the highest mountains. The Mariana Trench in the Pacific Ocean is 6.83 miles deep, over a mile deeper than Mount Everest is high. At that depth there are eight tons of water pressing down on each square inch, an unbearable environment. It is easier to map Mars than the seabed, and more people have been into space than into the great depths of the ocean. We may think we know our planet, but vast volumes of pitch dark soaking secrets are inaccessible still.

When we sunbathe on the beach, stroll along the shore, cross the Channel or swim in the sea, we are enjoying something that above all reveals the impenetrable, awesome, primitive power and glory of God. Jesus' disciples in the boat on the relatively tame Sea of Galilee appreciated this, which is why his command of the waves impresses and scares them in equal measure.

We often fail to remember this, seeing the seaside as a place of leisure and natural beauty. It is, of course, both; the lapping of waves upon a sun-soaked shore welcomes us to play in the shallows, while the roaring waves in a winter storm lashing the sea walls causes us to stand back in admiration. With feet on firm ground we truly can admire the works of the Lord from a safe distance.

Much of what we buy spends at least part of its journey to us on a ship. Huge container ships carry clothes, toys, cooking pots, cars and so much more to our shores. During the coronavirus pandemic much importing of goods was prevented or delayed, particularly in the early days when so much was sent from China, where the virus had first taken hold. The blocking of the Suez Canal by a stranded container ship in 2021 compounded the problem, as vessels queued up for weeks. Ports were closed, ships stranded and crews were abandoned to fend for themselves wherever they were.

Seafarers have difficult and dangerous lives at the best of times, yet during the pandemic their plight was barely mentioned, isolated as they were, either at sea or in strange lands. In April 2020, 200,000 cruise ship staff were stranded by the pandemic, unable to go home or set foot ashore. Similarly we may recall the cruise ships where the virus took hold and which were therefore denied entry to ports. The Braemar and the Zaandam were just two, on the latter of which four elderly passengers died at sea. Leisure passengers, who had no doubt paid serious money for a luxury cruise, discovered the tense fear of being imprisoned at sea and the futility of complaint.

The sea is not a virus, of course, yet it is noteworthy that the language of 'waves' of infection, rhythmically crashing in on us, has become common currency. The waves of Covid-19 have not ceased, and perhaps they never will. Like King Cnut, who reputedly sat on the seashore and tried to command the waves, attempts to control the coronavirus have met with frustration in the face of futility. Yet it was the same Cnut who, as his feet got wet, leapt up and according to the Chronicler Henry of Huntingdon, proclaimed, 'Let all the world know that the power of kings is empty and worthless, and there is no king worthy of the name save him by whose will heaven, earth and the sea obey eternal laws.'

Although that was a thousand years ago, it is still true, and whatever waves we are resisting, we need to remember that it is to Christ we should appeal and God in whom we trust.

O Christ, who stilled the storms and commanded the waves, hear the cries of your people rising and falling by the waves of disaster, famine or disease. Grant that in all circumstances we may recognise you, guiding and caring for us through the tumults of life until we reach the heavenly haven, where you welcome us as ruler of heaven and earth. Amen

25 Beaches

After these things Jesus showed himself again to the disciples by the Sea of Tiberias; and he showed himself in this way. Gathered there together were Simon Peter, Thomas called the Twin, Nathanael of Cana in Galilee, the sons of Zebedee, and two others of his disciples. Simon Peter said to them, 'I am going fishing.' They said to him, 'We will go with you.' They went out and got into the boat, but that night they caught nothing.

Just after daybreak, Jesus stood on the beach; but the disciples did not know that it was Jesus. Jesus said to them, 'Children, you have no fish, have you?' They answered him, 'No.' He said to them, 'Cast the net to the right side of the boat, and you will find some.' So they cast it, and now they were not able to haul it in because there were so many fish. That disciple whom Jesus loved said to Peter, 'It is the Lord!' When Simon Peter heard that it was the Lord, he put on some clothes, for he was naked, and jumped into the lake. But the other disciples came in the boat, dragging the net full of fish, for they were not far from the land, only about a hundred yards off...

When they had finished breakfast, Jesus said to Simon Peter, 'Simon son of John, do you love me more than these?' He said to him, 'Yes, Lord; you know that I love you.' Jesus said to him, 'Feed my lambs.' A second time he said to him, 'Simon son of John, do you love me?' He said to him, 'Yes, Lord; you know that I love you.' Jesus said to him, 'Tend my sheep.' He said to him the third time, 'Simon son of John, do you love me?' Peter felt hurt because he said to him the third time, 'Do you love me?' And he said to him, 'Lord, you know everything; you know that I love you.' Jesus said to him, 'Feed my sheep.'

JOHN 21:1–8, 15–17

During pandemic lockdowns, when very little social activity was permitted, many people were able to take to natural surroundings to experience some form of freedom. Swimming in the sea or walking on the shore were never forbidden. For those who could, particularly in the UK with its 7,723 miles of coastline, the sea gave an outlook to the beyond, not only to places across the sea, but also to a wider horizon of freedom from coronavirus confinement. Travelling on the sea to other countries was complicated, if allowed, but there was no law preventing the travel of the imagination and the healing rhythms of the song of the seashore. While the sea can be terrifying – as Bible stories such as Jesus calming the storm remind us – the beach is a very different place. The beach is a safe threshold, bordering the unknown, where the risen Jesus met his friends, ate with them and restored them to fellowship and pastoral purpose. He called his disciples on the beach; he said both 'Hello' and 'Farewell' on the Galilean shore.

The beach is the place where the twice-daily liturgies of the sea wash up, leaving the marks of God's creative power for all to see. Whether it is crabs in rockpools, strewn seaweed or coastal erosion, the beach reveals the constant yet changing patterns of ancient and modern tides, lapping or crashing on the land, pushed and pulled by the distant power of the perfectly placed moon. Unlike any other place on earth, the beach is where we can so easily see how God has put everything in order; it is a place where, as the poet John Donne put it, there are 'no ends nor beginnings, but one equal eternity'. To walk on a beach is to edge up to God's creative power, to dip one's toes in divine energy, orderliness and love.

It is on the beach that Jesus tested Peter's love three times and then instructed him to 'feed' his sheep. This restorative conversation is utterly pastoral. It is about how the love of Christ is to be taken beyond the beach, out into the seas of faith and hope which will ebb and flow forevermore. This love is not beach-bound; it is not brotherly love (*philia*), the word Peter uses, but rather *agape*, a distinctly Christian form of love that affirms and seeks the good of the other.

It is not sexual, possessive, jealous or familial. Jesus has to ask Peter three times, using the word *agape*, and only on the third time does Peter reply with this word rather than *philia*.

The linguistically hidden message is clear: Christian faith and pastoral care are built not only on brotherhood but life-affirming, boundary-breaking compassion which looks out for the well-being and flourishing of individuals and communities. This groundbreaking redefinition of love took place at the Galilean seaside, eroding fear and selfishness and changing the world forever. Interestingly, in the modern, culturally Christian Greek language, it is *agape* that has survived as the main word for 'love', even though ancient and first-century Greek had several other, more nuanced words.

The love of God found on the beach is also fundamentally trinitarian. Not only do we have the creative power of the sea remoulding coastlines daily and the remembrance of pastoral caring love at that beach breakfast, we also think of the Spirit of God moving upon the waters at creation and inspiring Christians ever since. The waves beating on the shore can be spiritual waves, too, ebbing and flowing in our lives like tides of divine presence reliably and regularly shaping us and directing our journeys of faith. Paradoxically, we believe in free will – that we are the drivers of our own destiny – yet simultaneously seek God's providence, guidance and sustenance. On the beach we encounter both sides of this apparent contradiction, random patterns in the sand that remind us of God, the creator, lover and redeemer, who gives the universe both freedom and purpose. In grains of sand and tidal waves alike, this freedom of the universe is revealed in beauty and truth: a sign of free grace given to all by God's Holy Spirit.

So next time you are on a beach, experiencing the vast distance of sand, stone and sea, come close to God, who in love and freedom guides, releases and calls us to be his own.

God our spiritual shepherd, who has numbered the grains of sand on the shore and every hair of our heads, we thank you for the raging of the sea and the serenity of the beach. Guide us through the tides of life, that we may never be cut off from your love, for you are God, Father, Son and Holy Spirit, Trinity in unity. Amen

26 Sand

> 'Everyone then who hears these words of mine and acts on them will be like a wise man who built his house on rock. The rain fell, the floods came, and the winds blew and beat on that house, but it did not fall, because it had been founded on rock. And everyone who hears these words of mine and does not act on them will be like a foolish man who built his house on sand. The rain fell, and the floods came, and the winds blew and beat against that house, and it fell – and great was its fall!'
>
> Now when Jesus had finished saying these things, the crowds were astounded at his teaching, for he taught them as one having authority, and not as their scribes.

MATTHEW 7:24–29

Sand is a strange substance. Its weakness is its strength, and its strength is its weakness. On a beach, sand can blow in your face, but it can also form a hard surface on which to walk – or, where the waves have just gone out, be soft enough for your feet to sink into. Sand comes in many colours and is composed in varying ways, depending on the locality. The most common ingredient of sand is silicon dioxide in the form of quartz. Sand is used to make glass, and some sand is made up of calcium carbonate, created over hundreds of millions of years by dead life forms such as coral and shellfish.

Sand represents the fundamental fragility of our lives. It is so easily washed or blown away and anything constructed with sand can disappear in a moment. Even if a structure lasts, it constantly erodes, as anyone who has built a sandcastle knows well. This process is known as entropy. The wisdom of Jesus' words about not building a house

on sand is not in doubt; they come at the end of the sermon on the mount, which he delivered by the Sea of Galilee, probably standing on a rocky outcrop. As he concluded his outdoor sermon, the crowds were surrounded by sand and rock and sky and sea. So his illustration was simple and plain: just as a house needs to be built on a strong and sound base, so too faith needs to be built on strong stuff that does not blow away or tend towards entropy. How true this is still today. Entropy is a measurable physical property commonly associated with a state of disorder, randomness or uncertainty. Whether or not Jesus knew the laws of thermodynamics, his message is spot on: sand is weak, do not build on it.

Yet sand is an ingredient of one of the strongest substances we can make. Mixed with cement and gravel it makes concrete – the most widely used material in existence (we use only water in greater quantities). The technique is not new – the Babylonians, Assyrians and Romans all made early forms of concrete by binding sand and lime. The Colosseum in Rome was largely built from it (which may be why it still stands today). Yet sand, copious as it is, is a non-renewable substance, and the manufacture of cement and concrete produces eight per cent of global greenhouse gas emissions. If we could find better building materials, the future of the planet would be built on better foundations.

There is a lot of sand in the world. When God blessed Abraham, he said, 'I will indeed bless you, and I will make your offspring as numerous as the stars of heaven and as the sand that is on the seashore' (Genesis 22:17). Jacob reminded God of that promise: 'You have said, "I will surely do you good, and make your offspring as the sand of the sea, which cannot be counted because of their number"' (Genesis 32:12). When Joseph's harvest succeeded, he abandoned counting the grain because it was 'like the sand of the sea… beyond measure' (Genesis 41:49). The psalmist says God's thoughts are even more numerous than the sand (Psalm 139:18). It makes us wonder, how many grains of sand are there? And how many people?

Sand grains were defined by Archimedes, around 240BC, as being 0.02 mm in diameter. One square metre of beach down to a depth of three metres might hold about 163 billion grains of sand. This makes the number of grains of sand on a beach incalculable. Yet science writer David Blatner has tried: assuming a grain of sand has an average size, and one calculates how many grains are in a teaspoon and then multiplies this by all the beaches and deserts in the world, the earth has very roughly seven quintillion, five hundred quadrillion (7,500,000,000,000,000,000) grains of sand. Meanwhile the Population Reference Bureau reckons that since humanity came into existence there have been 117 billion people born. Some 7.8 billion are alive now, which is seven per cent of all those who have ever lived.

Like houses built on or of sand, we are subject to entropy. That anything made of sand disintegrates quickly, leaving nothing behind, is a sign and symptom of our earthly existence. We are like sand, formed into beautiful shapes and patterns perhaps, but nevertheless subject to the winds and tides of time, which bears us away with solemn certainty and efficiency. We should not build our lives on dusty sand because we *are* sand – we were made from dust and to dust we shall return. When war, famine, natural disaster or a viral pandemic takes many lives, our fragility and our temporality on earth become acute, reflected by the glassy sand on which we walk and with which we build our houses.

Sand, by its very nature and the uses to which it may be put, reflects back to us faith, hope and love. Something so small and apparently fragile and insignificant can contribute to strong foundations and towering edifices. That such a weak and flimsy material as sand can be one of the ingredients of such strength reminds us of the life and love of Christ. Jesus gave up his divine power in the weakness of submission to death on the cross. The meaning of his words in Galilee is that he, Jesus Christ, is the foundation of our faith, and we build on him and him alone. He is the rock, and we, like the numerous grains of sand on the shore, need to be cemented to him, so that our hope is secure, our faith firm and our love eternal.

Jesus, who in turning your divine power into human weakness gave us the strength to live and the hope of resurrection life, endow the brevity of our existence with a greater glory, a surer faith and the assurance of your eternal love, now and always. Amen

27 Autumn leaves

In the beginning when God created the heavens and the earth, the earth was a formless void and darkness covered the face of the deep, while a wind from God swept over the face of the waters. Then God said, 'Let there be light'; and there was light…

Then God said, 'Let the earth put forth vegetation: plants yielding seed, and fruit trees of every kind on earth that bear fruit with the seed in it.' And it was so. The earth brought forth vegetation: plants yielding seed of every kind, and trees of every kind bearing fruit with the seed in it. And God saw that it was good. And there was evening and there was morning, the third day.

And God said, 'Let there be lights in the dome of the sky to separate the day from the night; and let them be for signs and for seasons and for days and years, and let them be lights in the dome of the sky to give light upon the earth.'

GENESIS 1:1–3, 11–15

The changing colour of leaves is a natural process. For leaves are not green: their natural colours are orange, yellow, gold or brown. The green we see comes from chlorophyll, the pigment that plants need to convert carbon dioxide and water, using sunlight, into oxygen and glucose, a process known as photosynthesis. Without this remarkable and seemingly miraculous process, most other lifeforms could not exist. Photosynthesis ignites and illuminates the whole food chain.

We might say that the divine imperative 'Let there be light' set in motion a chain reaction, whereby the light of God sustains life through a biochemical process without which, nothing.

In climates where sunlight varies through the year, there are periods – autumn and winter – when the light fades and the production of chlorophyll cannot be sustained in a large organism such as a tree. A deciduous tree cannot make enough food for itself, so it shuts down, and the chlorophyll drains from its green leaves, revealing their true colours underneath. As the chlorophyll fails, the tree produces anthocyanins, which produce a red colour. At different stages of its life cycle, a tree can have green, yellow, orange or red leaves. Some trees produce anthocyanins more quickly than others, so they miss out some of these colours, which is why in autumn there is a vast diversity to beguile the eye. Nevertheless, the leaves do eventually die, turn brown and fall.

During the Covid-19 pandemic, the artist Peter Walker created an installation entitled *The Leaves of the Trees*, which went on display in several cathedrals. It was composed of 5,000 steel leaves, each with the word 'hope' stamped into it, laid out like fallen autumn leaves. Over time the steel changed colour as it rusted. Symbolising past loss but also hope for the future, the artwork was intended to aid reflection on the pandemic period, in memory not only of those who died or lost loved ones, but also those who had been affected in any way; that is, all of us. The steel leaves can be seen as dead leaves that have fallen, to decay and rust on the ground, to return to earth.

Just as real leaves need to convert carbon dioxide into oxygen to feed themselves through the process of photosynthesis, so too is rusting a process of oxidisation. The iron in the steel reacts with the oxygen and water present in the air to create iron oxide. When a piece of metal rusts, carbonic acid is formed, which dissolves the iron, and some of the water will break down into hydrogen and oxygen. The oxygen released blends with the dissolved iron, creating what we call rust.

Is the rusting of metal leaves, or the browning of natural leaves, something by which we may be comforted, inspired or confused? The coronavirus pandemic has left many scars and much death. Now that the rains of the pandemic have subsided a little, do we simply consign those years to floods of forgetfulness and move on, leaving our griefs, struggles and sorrows to quietly rust or decay into the ground? Does this rust reflect the passing of time, over which everything decays – a process known as entropy? From dust we came and to dust we shall return. Do we, like Job, ask, 'Remember that you fashioned me like clay; and will you turn me to dust again?' (Job 10:9). Are we to remember, like the psalmist, that:

> You turn us back to dust,
>   and say, 'Turn back, you mortals.'
> For a thousand years in your sight
>   are like yesterday when it is past,
>   or like a watch in the night.
> You sweep them away; they are like a dream,
>   like grass that is renewed in the morning;
> in the morning it flourishes and is renewed;
>   in the evening it fades and withers.
>
> PSALM 90:3–6

Fallen leaves blowing in the wind and decaying on the ground – or metallic leaves rusting – ask us these questions, and query life itself. They expose us to the faith which may have been challenged or the love we have shared and perhaps lost, and they confront us with what happens if we lose hope. Yet they may also remind us of the words of the apostle Paul, who speaks of the 'hope that the creation itself will be set free from its bondage to decay and will obtain the freedom of the glory of the children of God' (Romans 8:20–21).

When we see leaves on the ground, we are reminded of the natural processes of creation and of the nourishment of plant and animal life, and that 'the leaves of the tree are for the healing of the nations' (Revelation 22:2). We are also reminded that all leaves revert to their natural state, drop and decay, their russet colours dissolving into the ground. Yet there is the hope of another year, another rebirth, another resurrection. Year by year we welcome spring, and (in the northern hemisphere) the joy of Easter resurrection that accompanies it. Whatever has happened, we can look back with reflective sorrow, as is both natural and right, and inoculate our beloved memories from the rust of despair; but we also look to the photosynthetic light of Christ, who daily feeds our beautiful multicoloured bodies and souls with the glorious hope of resurrection life.

Creator God, whose heavenly leaves of the trees are for the healing of the nations, hear us as we contemplate the challenges of recent years. We hold before you all who have died or whose lives changed forever. Give us grace to look back with love, to journey in faith and live in hope, for the sake of the Prince of Peace, Jesus Christ. Amen

28 Anger and abuse

The Passover of the Jews was near, and Jesus went up to Jerusalem. In the temple he found people selling cattle, sheep, and doves, and the money-changers seated at their tables. Making a whip of cords, he drove all of them out of the temple, both the sheep and the cattle. He also poured out the coins of the money-changers and overturned their tables. He told those who were selling the doves, 'Take these things out of here! Stop making my Father's house a market-place!' His disciples remembered that it was written, 'Zeal for your house will consume me.' The Jews then said to him, 'What sign can you show us for doing this?' Jesus answered them, 'Destroy this temple, and in three days I will raise it up.' The Jews then said, 'This temple has been under construction for forty-six years, and will you raise it up in three days?' But he was speaking of the temple of his body.

JOHN 2:13–21

There is another virus among us, which may well outlive Covid-19. It has certainly been around a long time. It gets into our bodies, flows through our veins, inflames our arteries and messes with our heads. It damages mental health, deprives people of sleep and can cause violent physical reactions and even death. It is infectious, virulent and to some extent incurable. It brings on increased levels of adrenaline and affects body movement, facial expression and even language. It has so many variants that there is no point even trying to vaccinate against it; rather, it has to be managed. The word for it originates in the Old Norse language – anger. We have all had it from time to time, and none of us is immune.

There has been much anger about all sorts of things in national and international life in recent years. Politicians' behaviour, fiscal policy, wars, the suppression of human rights – all these upset us.

Meanwhile behind closed doors, a whole range of passive and aggressive anger becomes available – cold shoulders and sulking, the undermining of others' achievements, psychological manipulation, constant criticism, bullying, abuse and violence. During the Covid-19 pandemic, it became clear that the hidden virus of domestic violence and abuse was spreading too. So much, in fact, that in October 2020 the United Nations called for a 'ceasefire' in response to what Secretary-General António Guterres called a horrifying global surge in domestic violence. In the UK, the charities Refuge and Respect both reported significant increases in calls concerning domestic violence against women and men. It took the pandemic to wake up the world to this. There is a lot more pent-up anger released violently in homes than many of us imagined.

Reading this, you could be a victim yourself or perhaps a perpetrator. Or you might know someone who is – the numbers of folk affected is staggering. Similarly with other forms of abuse; some say one in six people are affected by sexual abuse during their lifetimes. This might well, indeed it should, make us angry.

Not only should we be angry – in a rational, controlled, active way – about the abuse that is inflicted on so many people in so many ways (emotional, psychological, physical, sexual or exploitative); we should also be especially angry at the way we ignore victims and survivors of such abuse. There are victims and survivors of domestic, sexual and institutional abuse in churches, clubs, youth organisations, schools, children's homes, workplaces, sports clubs and media organisations – indeed, all around us.

Recent years have revealed a catalogue of disaster, irresponsibility and negligence, which extends into carelessness, disrespect and even cruelty of its own. One of the main burdens of being a survivor of abuse is the mountain of disbelief that so many do not have the inner strength or ability to climb. So many suffer in the silence of despondency, defeated by the system. And they do so because they say organisations such as churches are not taking them seriously. No wonder people are angry.

Jesus would be too. He turned the tables over and cast out the temple priests for exploiting the pilgrims who went up to Jerusalem to celebrate the Passover. It was exploitation – financial abuse of those who had no choice but to buy what was being sold and pay the price demanded. The temple priests had a monopoly on supplying 'unblemished' lambs for Passover meals, and it is this exploitation that Jesus criticises when turning the tables on them. His action was politically powerful, religious dynamite, the repercussions of which still reverberate today. One of those repercussions, which the church has largely failed to see and has been rightly criticised for, is failing to notice what Jesus says and does to those who abuse others. Jesus turned the tables on abusers. He kicked them out.

The church, local and global, cannot carry on not taking sides. The barriers have come down; there is no fence to sit on anymore. Sometimes we have to take sides. It is simply not true to say that Jesus did not take sides. This passage reveals that he took a side – took a stand – against those who exploited others for their own pleasure and gain. He took a stand against sin, and an even bigger stand when he submitted to a world of sin from the cross.

What we see in all this, is humble anger. Humble anger involves a paradoxical blend of humility and anger. It involves a recognition of worthlessness, failure and repentance, combined with a humble angry resolution to turn the tables on past wrongs, to retune to the voices of victims and survivors in a spirit of sorrow, remorse and submission. As we resume our lives in an emerging world, let us all be more alert to, and resolve to alleviate, some of the terrible things that God's children have done and still do to one another, meeting it with anger and humility.

Father God, who looks on sin with grief and horror and weeps with those who are damaged by the destructive actions of others, give us courage, determination, compassion and humility to watch out, speak out and help out where there is suffering, exploitation and evil. Amen

29 Friends and family

This is my commandment, that you love one another as I have loved you. No one has greater love than this, to lay down one's life for one's friends. You are my friends if you do what I command you. I do not call you servants any longer, because the servant does not know what the master is doing; but I have called you friends, because I have made known to you everything that I have heard from my Father. You did not choose me but I chose you. And I appointed you to go and bear fruit, fruit that will last, so that the Father will give you whatever you ask him in my name. I am giving you these commands so that you may love one another.

JOHN 15:12–17

What is a friend? What is it to be someone's friend? An important manifestation of friendship is spending 'face time' together in a relaxed environment, to be able to share your thoughts and opinions, hopes and fears, news and gossip; to offer advice, comfort, consolation and encouragement; and to speak truth, as perhaps no one else can. For several months in 2020, the only unmasked face time one could participate in involved the use of technology. Apple even calls its video-calling app FaceTime. So 'facetime' became a verb – to have a private one-to-one on screen.

WhatsApp and Facebook do the same. Facebook – again, the idea that friendship involves faces. Famously, Facebook also invented a new kind of online friend, involving the verb 'to friend', or even, to 'unfriend'. (Although 'unfriend' is actually a Middle English word from Chaucer's day and is useful as a noun, too – an 'unfriend' is an enemy.)

Meanwhile Shakespeare reminds us in *Romeo and Juliet* that while one's family included everyone under the same roof, it was actually one's 'friends' who were blood relatives.

Nowadays the words have almost been reversed, although some organisations use the word 'family' in a friendly, inclusive way of describing a group of people with common interest who love and look after one another. We can speak of the Scouting family, and, as in many communities, the 'church family'.

Church 'families' were dispersed and divided by Covid-19. Church is the family of God, friends with and under Christ. Yet there is no sub-stitute for being together under the nave roof, journeying together in an ark of faith. For many that journey through the choppy waters of the pandemic was a shared one, albeit online, and now church communities have landed on shores that are both familiar and new.

They landed *together* – that is what is important. Christians land as those who have a friend in Jesus, friends in Christ who have been on a stormy journey, together. They did not forget their friends, and It was good to see them again, to have friends and to hold them.

We use the language of 'having' friends, and there is an important sense in which that 'having' translates as a form of ownership or possession. We 'own' our friends, and they own us. Our ownership consists in the sharing of experiences and values. Sharing is a kind of mutual owning, for what we share in friendship we jointly own. While we have our friends we rejoice with them, not only because friendship is a gift from God exemplified in Christ, but also because, as Ralph Waldo Emerson put it: 'A friend may well be reckoned the masterpiece of nature.'

Jesus called his disciples friends, even though they caused him pain as well as joy. He called his disciples friends, but this encompasses the suffering, rejection and betrayal which they will not only endure together for each other's sake, but also do to each other when they are at their most vulnerable, weak and desolate. True friendship involves all of these dimensions: love, rejection, fear, doubt, the crucifixion of betrayal and the resurrection of forgiveness. This is worth remembering, because during the pandemic, we may have lost touch with, felt abandoned by, or even felt betrayed by our friends in some sense. Covid-19 has damaged as well as redefined friendship to some extent.

The disciples also in a sense owned each other – trusted each other – with part of themselves. When Jesus gave part of himself to Peter, for instance, he had to trust him – but then Peter let him down, denying that they were friends. This must be the hardest thing: when someone whom you consider to be your friend denies even knowing you. It is what Peter did to Jesus, and to some extent it is also what so many of us do to God sometimes. We keep quiet about our faith, seeking not to offend or hiding from challenge or controversy. We often do not speak up for Jesus. In Christ, God has made himself vulnerable to be in relationship with his creation, yet we have some inclination to disown, deny or even denounce him. God has given us something that is part of himself – a divine spark if you like – and this is what we do with it.

As Jesus was vulnerable with his friends, so it is with us. We too can and do give one another parts of ourselves. Yet we do not often hear people say, 'What have you done with that part of me I gave you?' This is because if we give someone something, they own it from then on. They only cease to own it if they throw it away or lose it. And in such carelessness lies the vulnerability that comes with giving and sharing. In the best of friendship there is fragility too. The greater the friendship, the higher the cost of betrayal.

As baptised friends of Christ, we belong to one other within the family of God. Belonging is very important – we belong to places, to our family and to our friends, and they belong to us. The language of possession is appropriate. We belong to each other – us and God, and also you and I. The basis of that belonging is love. And the chief symptom of love is friendship.

God, our Father and friend, may we all abide in your love and enjoy the fellowship of your family in and with Christ until our lives' end. Amen

30 Halloween

And what more should I say? For time would fail me to tell of Gideon, Barak, Samson, Jephthah, of David and Samuel and the prophets – who through faith conquered kingdoms, administered justice, obtained promises, shut the mouths of lions, quenched raging fire, escaped the edge of the sword, won strength out of weakness, became mighty in war, put foreign armies to flight. Women received their dead by resurrection. Others were tortured, refusing to accept release, in order to obtain a better resurrection. Others suffered mocking and flogging, and even chains and imprisonment. They were stoned to death, they were sawn in two, they were killed by the sword; they went about in skins of sheep and goats, destitute, persecuted, tormented – of whom the world was not worthy. They wandered in deserts and mountains, and in caves and holes in the ground.

Yet all these, though they were commended for their faith, did not receive what was promised, since God had provided something better so that they would not, apart from us, be made perfect.

Therefore, since we are surrounded by so great a cloud of witnesses, let us also lay aside every weight and the sin that clings so closely, and let us run with perseverance the race that is set before us, looking to Jesus the pioneer and perfecter of our faith, who for the sake of the joy that was set before him endured the cross, disregarding its shame, and has taken his seat at the right hand of the throne of God.

HEBREWS 11:32—12:2

Halloween flavours late October, with everything from chocolate treats to pumpkin tricks on sale in corner shops and supermarkets. Millions of pounds will be made on the back of a broomstick. But we must not be tricked by these treats. The eve of All Hallows is a slightly archaic name for the Eve of All Saints' Day, Hallow e'en. The eve of a saint's day is traditionally associated with the first service of the saint: the evening prayer on the day before can and often is associated with a vigil in anticipation of the following feast day. Christmas Eve is the obvious parallel. So the eve of All Saints' Day is a celebration of all the saints, especially of all the saints who do not have specific feast days of their own.

We are all saints, the 'holy people of God'. The psalmist describes the saints as 'all you who wait for the Lord' (Psalm 31:24), Matthew writes of the 'saints' who were raised when Jesus died (Mathew 27:52), and in Acts 9 there are three references to fellow, living saints. Paul uses this language in his letters to Rome, Corinth, Ephesus, Philippi, Colossae and Thessalonica, as well as in personal letters to Timothy and Philemon. Jude and the writer of Revelation also use the term copiously. Most significant is this passage from the letter to the Hebrews, which puts this idea into the context of a catalogue of holy people who did not know the Lord Jesus, but who heralded a tradition in which we as Christian 'saints' are in communion. This 'cloud of witnesses' surrounds us still, and amid that throng we are united with those whom we still love but see no longer. When we pray or sing, we do so in union with them and our worship ascends with theirs to the throne of God.

All Saints' tide includes, on 2 November, the more sombre festival of All Souls' Day. All Souls' Day has been reclaimed by the church in recent years as an opportunity to remember and celebrate the lives of those whom we love but see no longer. During and after the Covid-19 pandemic, it has gained a special poignancy and relevance, not least because for two years it was subdued by the tiers of lockdown alongside the tears of mass loss. The tradition in some churches of reading aloud the names of those who have died has deep pastoral and prayerful power. We remember before God those who dwell in a greater light. All Saints' Day is a day of holy celebration and All Souls' Day, one of great comfort.

This is far removed from the 21st-century secular Halloween, super-imposed on these holy days, which, often coinciding with schools' half-term break, can involve treats or 'tricks' of unkind pranks, which might include throwing eggs at doors or people. Not all the fun is harmless. For sainthood and remembrance are located in love of God and of others. Halloween as we see and experience it in shops, on the streets and in the media is very different. It does not express gratitude, solidarity or hope for those who have died, and death becomes a kind of joke, trivialised and reduced to silly costumes.

Some church communities attempt to reclaim Halloween and hold a festival of light, focusing on the light of Christ in which the saints are forever bathed. For there is fun to be had in light, rather than darkness. Seasonal pumpkins are indeed tasty, but do not need to be carved into scary faces. Instead we might be reminded of the face of Jesus Christ, whose light shines in the face of every human being.

As this time of remembrance comes round again, beginning with the celebration of All Hallows, pray for those who celebrate evil, know-ingly or otherwise, and remember all the saints who have died, of Covid or otherwise, and who reign with Christ in the glory of God the Father, by whose Spirit our praise and worship joins with theirs in heavenly light.

Holy Jesus, as we strive to be your saints on earth, look with pity on those without understanding and help us to witness to the light of your gospel, for you are holy, blameless, undefiled, separated from sinners and exalted above the heavens. Amen

31 Bonfires and fireworks

Let the same mind be in you that was in Christ Jesus,

who, though he was in the form of God,
    did not regard equality with God
    as something to be exploited,
but emptied himself,
    taking the form of a slave,
    being born in human likeness.
And being found in human form,
    he humbled himself
    and became obedient to the point of death –
    even death on a cross.

Therefore God also highly exalted him
    and gave him the name
    that is above every name,
so that at the name of Jesus
    every knee should bend,
    in heaven and on earth and under the earth,
and every tongue should confess
    that Jesus Christ is Lord,
    to the glory of God the Father.

Therefore, my beloved, just as you have always obeyed me,
not only in my presence, but much more now in my absence,
work out your own salvation with fear and trembling; for it is
God who is at work in you, enabling you both to will and to
work for his good pleasure.

Do all things without murmuring and arguing, so that you may be blameless and innocent, children of God without blemish in the midst of a crooked and perverse generation, in which you shine like stars in the world. It is by your holding fast to the word of life that I can boast on the day of Christ that I did not run in vain or labour in vain. But even if I am being poured out as a libation over the sacrifice and the offering of your faith, I am glad and rejoice with all of you – and in the same way you also must be glad and rejoice with me.

PHILIPPIANS 2:5–18

On Ascension Day, some churches set off a firework rocket to symbolise Jesus' departure heavenward 40 days after Easter. It is a cause of celebration, and the firework adds some spectacle to the occasion. Yet the origin of fireworks gives some pause for thought. Rockets originated in the second century BC for religious celebrations, but evolved into deadly weapons. While we may also think of space rockets, which, like those we launch on bonfire night, ascend heavenward, we might also be reminded of the rockets which have terrorised war-torn skies ever since Hitler's development of the V2 in 1944. Rockets can be launched from air, land or sea, hailing down fire and death from the skies on unsuspecting, innocent populations with devastating effect.

Some popular fireworks have alarming origins and remind us of the martyrdoms of early saints. The most famous is perhaps the Catherine wheel, named after St Catherine of Alexandria. A fourth-century girl of noble birth, she refused to marry the Emperor Maxentius because she considered herself to be a 'bride of Christ'. He was so incensed that he ordered her to be tortured by being splayed on a spiked breaking wheel. The wheel broke, but she was ultimately beheaded. Revered as a significant early female saint, her gruesome demise is remembered in a rotating firework, which, as Christ's light did in her, burns bright for a brief while before expiring.

Another Roman emperor, Nero, gave us the Roman candle. A notorious persecutor of Christians, he introduced a form of immolation which involved covering Christians in tar with an improvised wick on their heads, thereby giving the appearance of candles. Ignited at the feet, it was an appalling torture, which Nero apparently used to illuminate his garden parties.

In the second edition of *Foxe's Book of Martyrs*, it is recorded of the Reformation bishop Latimer that, being burned at the stake, he said, 'Be of good comfort, Master Ridley, and play the man; we shall this day light such a candle by God's grace in England as shall never be put out.' The remark resonates with Eusebius' account of the martyrdom of Polycarp in AD155.

It is poignant to remember all Christian martyrs shining like stars in the sky when we see these fireworks briefly burning, and remember the greater light in the cause of which they so horribly gave up their lives.

Bonfire Night falls on 5 November. The story of 'Remember, remember the fifth of November, gunpowder, treason and plot' is familiar, originating in the attempt to blow up parliament in 1605. James VI of Scotland, son of Mary, Queen of Scots, succeeded Elizabeth I in 1603, and although he had been baptised a Catholic, it was a Catholic plot to overthrow his parliament. The conspirators' attempt to plant gunpowder in the cellars was foiled and after a swift and efficient national manhunt, the perpetrators were rounded up, tortured and cruelly executed. 'Penny for the guy' and the macabre, commemorative tradition of burning an effigy of Guy Fawkes developed. The use of fireworks reminds us of what might have happened had the gunpowder ignited.

Most people, however, do not pay attention to the uncomfortable origins of Bonfire Night. Instead, firework displays extend over a two-week period, illuminating our skies with beautiful colours and explosions which would harrow any battlefield, enjoyed by perhaps half the population – the other half being pet owners who dread early November for the sake of their terrified animals. (That said, the Italian town of Collechio was the first to insist on 'silent' fireworks in 2015. There is yet hope of peace for pyrophobic pets.)

Nevertheless fireworks can be invigorating, and while the noises they make would be alarming in other contexts, they are associated with celebrations, weddings, anniversaries and royal jubilees. The Lord Mayor's Show in the City of London is followed by fireworks, and as the new year is welcomed worldwide, capital cities launch firework displays of increasing complexity, beauty and expense.

Fireworks rise heavenward and, shining through the gloom, point us to the skies. They are microstars, exploding, burning and dying in seconds, echoing the lifespan of any star, including our own sun. They grant us a sense of perspective as their shooting light blends with that of the stars light years away, illuminating both our smallness and our significance. We can put stars in the sky, momentarily: a divine spark igniting the intelligence, knowledge and enjoyment of life with which God has blessed us. The greatness of God's universal power can be glimpsed in the fireworks of a night sky and seen for real when that divine firework of creative, sustaining love rises again: the sun, 865,000 miles in diameter, 330,000 times more massive than the earth, burning at its core at 15 million degrees Celcius. It gives heat, light, life and hope at the dawning of each new, resurrection day.

Exalted Christ of heaven and earth, as we remember those who have burned bright as stars of martyrdom, keep us shining brightly until that day when every knee shall bow at your name and all your people be filled with the light of faith, hope and love. Amen

32 War memorials

Let us now sing the praises of famous men,
    our ancestors in their generations.
The Lord apportioned to them great glory,
    his majesty from the beginning.
There were those who ruled in their kingdoms,
    and made a name for themselves by their valour;
those who gave counsel because they were intelligent;
    those who spoke in prophetic oracles;
those who led the people by their counsels
    and by their knowledge of the people's lore;
    they were wise in their words of instruction;
those who composed musical tunes,
    or put verses in writing;
rich men endowed with resources,
    living peacefully in their homes –
all these were honoured in their generations,
    and were the pride of their times.
Some of them have left behind a name,
    so that others declare their praise.
But of others there is no memory;
    they have perished as though they had never existed;
they have become as though they had never been born,
    they and their children after them.
But these also were godly men,
    whose righteous deeds have not been forgotten;
their wealth will remain with their descendants,
    and their inheritance with their children's children.
Their descendants stand by the covenants;

> their children also, for their sake.
> Their offspring will continue forever,
> and their glory will never be blotted out.
> Their bodies are buried in peace,
> but their name lives on generation after generation.
> The assembly declares their wisdom,
> and the congregation proclaims their praise.

SIRACH (ECCLESIASTICUS) 44:1–15

Plagues and wars come and go, but we are never rid of either. In the past hundred years or so, we have made a habit of making sure we do not forget wars or those who fell victim to them. On 8 May 1919, an Australian journalist, Edward Honey, wrote to the *London Evening News* proposing that the first anniversary of the armistice at the end of the Great War be commemorated by several moments of silence. He had served, and been injured, in the British Army during the war and felt that, a year after the joyful celebration of Armistice in 1918, a silent commemoration of the sacrifices made and the lives lost would be more fitting. He proposed a five-minute silence.

In October 1919 King George V heard of a similar suggestion made to Sir Percy Fitzpatrick, and he made an official proclamation that at the hour when the Armistice came into force (the eleventh hour of the eleventh day of the eleventh month), there could be a two-minute suspension of normal activities so that 'the thoughts of everyone may be concentrated on reverent remembrance of the glorious dead'. A rehearsal was held in Buckingham Palace, to which Edward Honey was invited. The poppy was adopted as a symbol of remembrance in 1921, and in the UK the transition from marking Armistice Day on 11 November to Remembrance Sunday on the second Sunday of the month seems to date from 1942.

While war memorials became prevalent in towns and villages after the war ended in 1918, some are older. The minutes of the parochial church council of St Mary Magdalene in Enfield record that the suggestion to have a war memorial erected in the church was made and agreed in 1917, in anticipation of the war ending, to honour those who had already lost their lives. Prior to World War I, it was not common to name the fallen, but rather to record the event and the general loss of life. Other memorials, such as the one in St Paul's Cathedral lamenting the sinking of HMS Captain in 1870, record the names of those lost at sea, including a list of 'boys' lost.

The unique memorial wall at the west end of Rochester Cathedral records military campaigns that go back 200 years to Waterloo and beyond. Unusually, it records the names of not only those who died in battle, but also those who served. In that memorial, which pre-dates so many others by a century, there is a recognition of bravery, courage, commitment and service, as well as of suffering. Reading the names, the roll call of those who went and may have returned, there is a sense of their grief and suffering as the ones who saw, stood beside, and even went down beside, those who did not return. In mid-November we remember those who gave their lives – those who demonstrated that greater love that lays down its life for friends – but we less often remember those who died years later, unrecorded, but who took to their quiet graves the service they rendered, the sights they saw, the mental and physical damage they themselves sustained. So often they go unremembered *because* they came home.

The debt to those who came home is no less great. The lockdowns of 2020 inspired many to great acts of fundraising and service, and the generation that was so affected by Covid restrictions, but which was perhaps best prepared to endure them, was the generation that had seen World War II. One of the lovely dimensions of the story of Captain Sir Tom Moore, who raised so much money for charity during Covid lockdowns, was the blend of admiration for his charity efforts and general character, alongside a recognition that a war veteran had become a national treasure. As an old soldier who lived to 100, he represented so many who served, came home and got forgotten.

Rochester Cathedral's connection with the Royal Engineers goes back nearly 1,000 years. The corps dates back to William the Conqueror and Bishop Gundulf, the Norman architect who built Rochester Castle and Cathedral and the Tower of London. This makes Rochester their spiritual home, but it took a millennium before the cathedral and the Royal Engineers actually went into battle together, in 2020. It was a very different kind of engagement as the cathedral opened its doors to become a Covid testing centre, and it was the Royal Engineers who made that happen, establishing a bridgehead in the campaign against Covid in Kent, which at that time had just become associated with a new, more virulent variant of Covid, to which the county gave its name. The historic connection became a partnership of modern times, when a church and military unit united in common cause against an unseen enemy.

These and all the sacrifices and service of those who fought in all sorts of battles should not be forgotten, belittled, trivialised or downplayed. Whatever the 'enemy' is, effort, energy and expertise is needed, and people who possessed or lacked these qualities have been defeated, mourned and memorialised in various ways. After Covid, communities and families have found ways to remember and memorialise those whom they love but see no longer, some of whom have died in the service of others, as medics, public transport workers or care workers. The fields of battle against Covid are, like the fields of blood that have beset world history, locations of suffering, valour and sacrifice as well as of determination and victory. Through it all we give thanks to God for them all, and pray for all who grieve their loss.

God, who calls us to service in so many diverse ways, sometimes even to the point of death, receive our thanks for those who sacrificed their days for our tomorrows, and hear our prayers for all whom they left behind. Inspire us all with that greater love shown by Jesus on the cross, which leads to resurrection life, opened up for us by the same Jesus Christ, our Lord. Amen

33 Silence

There is a rebuke that is untimely,
    and there is the person who is wise enough to keep silent…
Some people keep silent and are thought to be wise,
    while others are detested for being talkative.
Some people keep silent because they have nothing to say,
    while others keep silent because they know when to speak.
The wise remain silent until the right moment,
    but a boasting fool misses the right moment.
Whoever talks too much is detested,
    and whoever pretends to authority is hated.

SIRACH (ECCLESIASTICUS) 20:1, 5–8

The composer John Cage wrote a piece called '4'33' in which the performer sits at a piano or other instrument and does nothing for that length of time. Known to some as the 'silent' piece, it is not silent at all, for, as the composer himself pointed out in his book entitled *Silence* (1961), there is no such thing as silence and even if one were in a soundproof room one would hear the sounds of one's own body. His 'silent' piece is actually a piece of sound organisation, providing the listener with the opportunity to listen to and pay attention to sounds that would otherwise be unnoticed. If we pay attention to silence, we discover that it does not exist.

Yet we do speak of silence, and we 'observe' silence frequently. At this time of year, especially, many observe two minutes' silence on Armistice Day, Remembrance Sunday or both. As we have seen, this is a tradition which dates back just over a century, when the observance of the eleventh hour of the eleventh day of the eleventh month began.

An inspiration for the two minutes' silence may well have been this passage from Ecclesiastes:

> There is…
> a time to tear, and a time to sew;
> a time to keep silence, and a time to speak;
> a time to love, and a time to hate;
> a time for war, and a time for peace.
> ECCLESIASTES 3:7–8

Added to this is the silence of lament:

> The elders of daughter Zion
> sit on the ground in silence;
> they have thrown dust on their heads
> and put on sackcloth;
> the young girls of Jerusalem
> have bowed their heads to the ground.
> LAMENTATIONS 2:10

Combine these two and we have a sense of how and why we bow our heads in silence in remembrance of the sacrifices, horrors and eternal recurrence of warfare, recalling not only soldiers but also civilians, who are so often the silent ones on the receiving end.

The observance of a minute or two of silence is not confined to November remembrance. Many now hold a minute of silence when someone has died in their organisation or, more recently, for the victims of the Covid-19 pandemic. The idea of memorials and silences has been imported into civilian life too. There is much wisdom in the keeping of silence, as Sirach, the author of Ecclesiasticus, reminds us.

Silence so often speaks louder than words. In his treatise on linguistic philosophy entitled *Tractatus Logico-Philosophicus*, Ludwig Wittgenstein, an Austrian philosopher who served on the Russian front in World War I, concludes with the proposition, 'Whereof one cannot speak, thereof one must be silent.' Philosophical logic aside, this is a sentiment we can well adopt for some of those deep matters of life which either transcend faith or which seem to be belittled by words. Sometimes in the face of grief, loss, suffering and anguish, there are no words. To keep silence is the loudest thing we can do, and in some contexts we do it together, as a family, community, nation, world. Silence transcends language, politics, even meaning.

There are other forms of silence, though. Silence is also a verb, and many people over the centuries, in and out of the church, have tried to silence those whose message, views or stories are inconvenient. Whether we are thinking of heresies, reformations or safeguarding failures, silence has been imposed, perhaps in misuse of Peter's words: 'For it is God's will that by doing right you should silence the ignorance of the foolish' (1 Peter 2:15). Secretive or imposed silence can be wicked.

Sometimes silence is not optional. We should not overlook the silence which belongs to those who cannot hear. While some choose to remain silent and to hear only ambient sounds that occur during respectful silences, others live in a silent world, aided only by lipreading and sign language. The winner of the 2021 series of *Strictly Come Dancing* – a staple of the autumn television season in the UK – was the deaf actress Rose Ayling-Ellis. In an episode that aired on Remembrance weekend, she included in her dance several seconds of silence, during which she and her partner continued dancing while the music stopped. Whether the connection was deliberate, it was striking and moving, as the national audience kept silence for her to dance, welcomed for a few seconds into the world of those who are deaf.

The same weekend saw the end of the COP26 conference at which serious conversations and debates had taken place about the future of the planet, some of which fell on metaphorically deaf ears, and it was all flanked by the two minutes' silence of 11 November and Remembrance Sunday.

Silence has many colours and flavours. So we might ask, what is silence *for*? It is clear that all of these silences are for *paying attention*, for *listening* – to others, to reason, to God. Whether we are paying attention to sacrifice and grief, to the futility or necessity of war, to the need for peace, to the plight of deaf people, to the victims of abuse, or to the word of God, we need silence in our lives. Without it everything is just noise. Once we have stopped to eliminate the noise, some golden silence can rule us, however briefly, to be replaced by a more ordered music, to which, perhaps, after all, we can learn to dance.

A deaf dancer teaches us that one does not need music to dance, nor grief to be silent. There can be joy in silence and always a balance to be had and held. Silent prayer is not just for sorrow, but for gratitude, awe and reverence too. The prophet Habakkuk recounts how 'the Lord is in his holy temple; let all the earth keep silence before him!' (2:20). This reminds us of the opening of the seventh seal: 'When the Lamb opened the seventh seal, there was silence in heaven for about half an hour. And I saw the seven angels who stand before God, and seven trumpets were given to them' (Revelation 8:1–2). Silence is not always quiet.

Silence is both dark and golden. It is necessary, valuable but dangerous. It can be public or secretive. We can rightly have mixed feelings about it and the uses to which it is put. There are times for different kinds of silence. Pay attention, and next time you are bidden to silence, or find yourself in its company, consider what it means, in faith, hope and love.

O God, who speaks in the sheer silences of our hearts, and knows the secrets of all, hear our prayers for all who suffer unheard, grieve alone or search for hope amid the clamour of this world. May your still, small voice lead, console and inspire us this and every day. Amen

34 Online shopping

When they came to the place that is called The Skull, they crucified Jesus there with the criminals, one on his right and one on his left…

One of the criminals who were hanged there kept deriding him and saying, 'Are you not the Messiah? Save yourself and us!' But the other rebuked him, saying, 'Do you not fear God, since you are under the same sentence of condemnation? And we indeed have been condemned justly, for we are getting what we deserve for our deeds, but this man has done nothing wrong.' Then he said, 'Jesus, remember me when you come into your kingdom.' He replied, 'Truly I tell you, today you will be with me in Paradise.'

It was now about noon, and darkness came over the whole land until three in the afternoon, while the sun's light failed; and the curtain of the temple was torn in two. Then Jesus, crying with a loud voice, said, 'Father, into your hands I commend my spirit.' Having said this, he breathed his last.

LUKE 23:33, 39–46

With the advent of Covid-19 lockdowns, internet shopping came into its own. With supermarkets trying to respond to a demand they could barely meet, it was a lifeline for some. Others settled into their sofas and spent liberally, getting everything delivered, from food to exercise equipment. Yet the decline of the high street and the rise of online shopping cannot be blamed on the exigencies of 2020, as the trend had already begun, epitomised by the rise of Black Friday and Cyber Monday.

Black Friday is the day after Thanksgiving, which in the US occurs on the fourth Thursday of November and commemorates the first harvest celebrated by the pilgrim fathers, who settled in America in 1620. It thus has overtones of Harvest Festival, generosity and nationhood, alongside what was overtly a religious festival giving thanks to God for the bounty bestowed to relieve want and famine. The traditional fare of turkey, cranberry sauce, brussels sprouts and sweet potatoes is akin to Christmas dinner, with added marshmallows and perhaps pumpkin or cherry pie for dessert.

When I worked at St Paul's Cathedral it was my pleasure and privilege to be responsible for the annual Thanksgiving Day Service which is held for the American expatriot community in London. By custom, the US ambassador attends and the US president's annual speech is delivered from the pulpit (as well as a sermon). It was a great festival, and for me at the time a cheap way of going to America for the day and eating a Thanksgiving dinner!

Black Friday follows, and it is a far less spiritual festival. It may have a hint of the original pilgrim fathers' celebrating the end of famine, but there is little financial famine to associate with Black Friday (except perhaps remembering those for whom it is an inaccessible spendfest of self-indulgence and extravagance). Black Friday is the day when the 'run-up to Christmas' truly begins, with bargains for a spending season which runs for a bit longer than Advent. While Advent can be about self-denial, the Christmas shopping season that begins on Black Friday is about the opposite, even if the spending is on others. Black Friday is about splashing out on bargains, getting a good deal and paying as low a price as possible. For some, however, it is a temptation to spend money they do not actually have.

Black Friday is then followed by its online shopping equivalent, Cyber Monday. Thus, like Easter, this post-Thanksgiving shopping festival extends for a long weekend. It is pure 'holiday' in the post-Christian sense of the word: holy day becomes holiday, and it is not about God, but about money. And we know we cannot serve both (Luke 16:13).

Perhaps we can at least be pleased that the Black Friday–Cyber Monday spending holidays have not displaced any genuine holy days.

The spiritual irony of Black Friday is clear when we note that the 'black' in the name is not intended as a negative; in financial parlance, being 'in the black' is a positive – as opposed to being 'in the red'. In Christ, God often reverses things or turns them upside down, and in the topsy-turvy world in which we now live, what might be thought of as a black day in history is called good. Good Friday was a black Friday, the day when the cross of Christ ran red with his blood spilled for humanity.

That black Friday was the good day on which the commodity of salvation was at its most expensive; it was not discounted as cheap grace, knocked down for sins at a bargain price. Christ's kingly sacrifice on the cross was costly, and the debt he paid was to die for. But the present he bought with his red blood on that black Friday was all for good – as in forever. As Sydney Carter put it in his famous song: 'I danced on a Friday when the sky turned black.'

If you found some bargains on Black Friday, or perhaps plan to shop online for more deals in the Christmas or New Year sales, remember that black Friday all those years ago when Christ bought us all a bargain that cannot be repaid by any human being. The same Jesus who, we pray, will remember us when we come into his kingdom.

Jesus, as we remember that good black Friday when you paid the price of sin, remember me when you come into your kingdom. Amen

Advent

35 Kindness

'When the Son of Man comes in his glory, and all the angels with him, then he will sit on the throne of his glory. All the nations will be gathered before him, and he will separate people one from another as a shepherd separates the sheep from the goats, and he will put the sheep at his right hand and the goats at the left. Then the king will say to those at his right hand, "Come, you that are blessed by my Father, inherit the kingdom prepared for you from the foundation of the world; for I was hungry and you gave me food, I was thirsty and you gave me something to drink, I was a stranger and you welcomed me, I was naked and you gave me clothing, I was sick and you took care of me, I was in prison and you visited me." Then the righteous will answer him, "Lord, when was it that we saw you hungry and gave you food, or thirsty and gave you something to drink? And when was it that we saw you a stranger and welcomed you, or naked and gave you clothing? And when was it that we saw you sick or in prison and visited you?" And the king will answer them, "Truly I tell you, just as you did it to one of the least of these who are members of my family, you did it to me."'

MATTHEW 25:31–40

In August 2021 the BBC and the University of Sussex launched a research project called *The Kindness Test*. Sixty thousand people took part, and the findings are fascinating. The survey reveals that

kindness is not rare at all, particularly among family and friends. This is no surprise, for as Jesus asked, 'Is there anyone among you who, if your child asks for bread, will give a stone?' (Matthew 7:9). We are naturally kind to our family and friends, and most acts of kindness occur in the home. Kindness is rarest, apparently, online, on public transport and in the street.

Of those surveyed, 43% said that someone was kind to them each day. This everyday kindness is generally experienced in response to a request. Other kind acts include opening doors for others, picking things up and doing little favours. Many also expressed 'concerned feelings' for those less fortunate than themselves. Personality makes a difference, it seems: extroverts are more likely not only to be kind to others, but also to have kindness shown to them. The more one talks to strangers, the more kindness one both receives and notices going on. People who regularly benefit from kindness or simply notice the kindness of others have better levels of well-being. The adage that being kind makes one feel good is evidently true.

Sadly, when asked what might hinder kindness, many said that they feared they might be misinterpreted. Many of those surveyed said that they did not have enough time to be as kind as they would like, and half said that social media had a part to play in that. This contrasts with a finding of the survey that suggests that wealth does not really impact on kindness. There is evidence, however, that women and people of faith are kinder than others. Interestingly, the authors of the survey offer this interpretation of that conclusion:

> Of course we have to rely on self-reports in this study, so there is a possibility that women and religious people feel that they ought to say that they are kind in order to look good. But plenty of people are prepared to admit they're not very generous, for example, and previous studies have shown that we are quite good at judging our own levels of kindness.

As Christians we strive not to judge others, nor ourselves (Matthew 7:1–5). It is a shame that when it appears that people of faith – or any group of people – seem kinder to others, we try to find a potentially dismissive reason for that. It is clearly the case, and we need no survey to tell us, that someone does not need to have faith to be kind. It is also not surprising that people of faith tend to be kind, and it might stem from a disposition, inspired by devotion and learned from scripture, that being kind to others is both a calling and outworking of Christianity, promoted by Jesus and the apostle Paul, among others. Jesus said, 'Love your enemies, do good to those who hate you, bless those who curse you, pray for those who abuse you' (Luke 6:27–28). We are called to be kind.

The Kindness Test also found that two-thirds of respondents said that the Covid pandemic seemed to have made people kinder. Just as personality type, faith or gender can make a difference, it seems that the circumstances and challenges of a pandemic both encouraged and enabled people to take more time both to be kind and to notice kindness. There is a resonance here of the ancient call to be kind and generous to the vulnerable: 'Render true judgements, show kindness and mercy to one another; do not oppress the widow, the orphan, the alien, or the poor; and do not devise evil in your hearts against one another' (Zechariah 7:9–10). Similarly, we remember Micah's question, 'What does the Lord require of you but to do justice, and to love kindness, and to walk humbly with your God?' (Micah 6:8).

Questions such as this prick our conscience and perhaps help us both notice and be the agents of the form of kindness revealed in mercy, justice and humility. It is humbling when others are kind to us, and to be kind to others is an act of humility. The adage that being kind makes us feel good needs updating – being kind *is* good, benefiting giver and receiver alike. As we enter the Advent season, we notice its major theme, which concerns how we are judged before God, epitomised by the parable of God judging the nations like sheep and goats. For the ultimate kindness has been offered by God in Jesus Christ, in whose saving death and resurrection we experience the greatest justice and mercy ever told.

It is therefore a daily humility neither too great nor too small, as God's chosen ones, holy and beloved, to clothe ourselves with 'compassion, kindness, humility, meekness, and patience' (Colossians 3:12). As a fruit of the Spirit, kindness is in good company: 'love, joy, peace, patience, kindness, generosity, faithfulness, gentleness, and self-control' (Galatians 5:22–23). Kindness is also a mark of the best form of love, allied to patience, truthfulness, hope and endurance, as Paul famously put it when writing to the Corinthian church (1 Corinthians 13:4–7).

So, while it is good to have a survey of kindness in the wake of the pandemic and heartening to see that humanity has a predilection to be kind, contrary to the nastiness and brutal behaviour with which our airtime is invaded, our calling and purpose as Christians is ever to 'love, not in word or speech, but in truth and action' (1 John 3:18). May we continue to be nothing if not kind in our dealings with others.

Generous God, who in great kindness sent your Son to redeem the world, humbling himself to death on a cross, give us the same mind that was in Christ, that in showing mercy and pity to others we may be counted worthy to serve you on earth and in heaven. Amen

36 Deliveries

In those days a decree went out from Emperor Augustus that all the world should be registered. This was the first registration and was taken while Quirinius was governor of Syria. All went to their own towns to be registered. Joseph also went from the town of Nazareth in Galilee to Judea, to the city of David called Bethlehem, because he was descended from the house and family of David. He went to be registered with Mary, to whom he was engaged and who was expecting a child. While they were there, the time came for her to deliver her child. And she gave birth to her firstborn son and wrapped him in bands of cloth, and laid him in a manger, because there was no place for them in the inn.

LUKE 2:1–7

The advent of online shopping is often attributed to the launches of Amazon and Ebay in the mid 90s. Both took advantage of the early growth in internet use, and they thrive still. Yet as is often the case, the organisations who succeed first are not necessarily those who invent the idea or the technology. The earliest online shopping involved the connection of a domestic television set to a computer via a telephone line and was pioneered in the UK by Michael Aldrich in 1979. He is likely one of the most important IT innovators that most people have not heard of, and his work paved the way for something that so many of us take for granted: to order something online and have it delivered in a matter of days. Online shopping began with airline tickets and chocolates before Amazon started selling books, and by now almost anything can be bought online. Even cars, shoes and fresh meat can be chosen, ordered, paid for and delivered with sufficient efficiency.

Most items can be returned if they are not suitable, do not fit, or are damaged or unwanted.

As the lockdown of March 2020 came into effect, what seemed like an extravagance or symptom of laziness or convenience became a lifeline to many. While physical shops were closed, online shopping boomed. Supermarkets, which had built up a good consumer base in grocery deliveries, suddenly found themselves overwhelmed with demand and some restricted their delivery services to the isolated, aged or vulnerable.

For a while it seemed that most of the traffic on the UK's quiet roads was delivery vans. Touch-free delivery was introduced and for some the delivery driver became one of the few people they saw. Meanwhile in some communities, food deliveries and shopping collections were undertaken by volunteers. Near where I lived, the local youth hostel closed and we borrowed a refrigerated van to collect the contents of their freezers to distribute to schools and vulnerable people. There were many amateur delivery drivers on the roads at that time, doing their bit to make sure no one was too isolated or did not have food. The coronavirus was little known about and much feared, so the door-step delivery from a friendly, albeit masked, face was very welcome.

Meanwhile the major delivery firms and online suppliers ramped up their offering, reorganised their schedules and employed many more drivers to take to the streets. There were supply-chain problems, but one of the main influences the pandemic has had on the UK is to further embed online shopping as a mainstream phenomenon. Allied to this is the practice of delivering takeaway food ready to eat, a carry out which someone else fetches and brings to you for a small fee. Meals on wheels, which used to be associated with elderly house-bound people, is now the cool way to not bother to cook. Perhaps these developments would have naturally evolved over time, but it seems that the pandemic accelerated some of those trends, which are now here to stay.

In whatever ways this affected you, whatever advantages or benefits you may have experienced personally, this phenomenon is worth reflecting on. Alongside the ability to summon at leisure whatever one desires comes the anticipation of its delivery. In the time between clicking the order online and the driver arriving at the door, in a sense a shadow falls. It is a period in which reflection can take place: *Did I really need that? When will it arrive? Shall I send it back?* This 'shadow' period is a time of waiting, anticipation, excitement even.

Advent is about waiting and anticipation, and about excitement. Advent calendars and pre-Christmas shopping and shipping creates an anticipatory excitement for the post to arrive. Father Christmas is, after all, a rather overloaded, supersonic, mythical delivery man who gets everything over the threshold or down the chimney in the allotted space–time continuum!

The anticipation of the delivery driver with their wares is therefore both an ancient and a modern phenomenon. It carries us back to the anticipation of a Messiah, held for centuries by the Hebrew people, which then, after the angel Gabriel had spoken to Mary, became a waiting period, literally a pregnant pause in salvation history. Between the idea planted by Gabriel and the reality of childbirth comes the shadow, the waiting, the doubting, the fearing, the wondering. It is a fundamentally human experience, for anyone awaiting a newborn. For anyone awaiting anything, in fact. There is darkness before delivery.

As we anticipate the celebration of the birth of Christ, it may feel routine, part of the seasonal cycle. Yet Christmases in the past few years have not been without their dark difficulties and restrictions. This highlights the fact that every time God delivers Christmas to us, it is both the same and different, familiar and strange. Like the delivery of the package we have ordered, we know what is inside, but it is exciting to open it nonetheless.

We did not order Christmas. We did not ask to be saved. God does not deliver Jesus to us on demand or because we have ticked a box or decided we would like it. Nor can we send him back. We can reject him knocking at the doors of our lives, seeking admission, but he will not go away unwanted, damaged, returned. Rather, he is the perfect gift of faith, hope and love. Sent and delivered without payment, undeserved and signed for only on the cross, the payment is made not *to* him, but *by* him. If there is a box to tick, it is the universal one that applies to us all – that we are sinners in need of redemption, light and hope. All of these burst forth when humanity receives and opens that tiny bundle delivered to the world on the first Christmas day, and every day since.

Thank you, God, for the annual delivery of Advent and Christmas, through which we are reminded of your loving mercy, incarnational presence and redemptive power which you bring to us in the person of Jesus Christ, who with you and by the Spirit is one God, Father, Son and Holy Spirit. Amen

37 Board games

Look at what is before your eyes. If you are confident that you belong to Christ, remind yourself of this, that just as you belong to Christ, so also do we. Now, even if I boast a little too much of our authority, which the Lord gave for building you up and not for tearing you down, I will not be ashamed of it. I do not want to seem as though I am trying to frighten you with my letters. For they say, 'His letters are weighty and strong, but his bodily presence is weak, and his speech contemptible.' Let such people understand that what we say by letter when absent, we will also do when present.

We do not dare to classify or compare ourselves with some of those who commend themselves. But when they measure themselves by one another, and compare themselves with one another, they do not show good sense. We, however, will not boast beyond limits, but will keep within the field that God has assigned to us, to reach out even as far as you. For we were not overstepping our limits when we reached you; we were the first to come all the way to you with the good news of Christ.

2 CORINTHIANS 10:7–14

Ever since Charles Dickens published *A Christmas Carol* in 1843 and made Christmas a family time of fun, festivity and financial friendship to the needy, Christmas has been a kind of 'destination' event at the end of the year. For the past few years, however, it has felt like we have struggled to make it there. In 2020 Christmas was effectively cancelled socially, and in 2021 it was a close-run thing – it is reckoned in that year that one million people in the UK were in isolation from having

contracted, or being close companions of those who had, the omicron variant of Covid-19. My family and I were among them.

Part of the festive fun of Christmas involves playing family games; Dickens himself was a fan of blind man's buff. But like a game of snakes and ladders, the coronavirus period felt like climbing a ladder only to slide down a slithery serpentine slope – two steps forward, one step back. Covid-19 and its variants are not a game, of course, but it did feel as though each Christmas was like trying to get to 'Go' (to use another well-known board game), only with all sorts of obstacles in the way. Many did not make it or limped there in quarantine or sickness. Christmas has always been a time that causes some people to feel isolated – the lonely, the aged, the unloved. Add to this medical isolation enforced by infection, contagion or contact, and many found themselves engulfed in the dark and lonely shadows of a Covid winter.

The analogy with games reminds us not only of the dicey nature of our relationship with a contaminating virus, but also of the fact that playing games is a natural, beneficial and enjoyable thing to do. Many Christmas traditions involve games, and in the second half of the 20th century the popularity of board games increased significantly. Chess, *Monopoly*, *Risk* and *Trivial Pursuit* are very much cultural objects, loved by so many people. We know what it is to 'pass Go' or to be 'checkmated', terms which have literal meaning in a game and metaphorical meaning in life.

The Mesopotamians had the table game of backgammon to play 5,000 years ago, and the ancient Egyptians played a game called *senet* around 3,500 years ago, which is the oldest known board game. In the *Iliad* (written by Homer in the 8th century BC), the ancient Greek game of *petteia* is mentioned. This game evolved into one the Romans played which they called *ludus latrunculorum*. The Latin word for 'play' is *ludo*, which is also the name of another game that, as it happens, is not Roman but based on an Indian sixth-century game called *pachisi*.

More recently, in 1843, a board game was released in the USA which sent players along a journey of virtues and vices that led to the 'mansion of happiness' (heaven). This may remind us of snakes and ladders, which was originally an ancient Indian board game called *moksha patam*. There is a biblical version of this game, known as *Bible Ups and Downs*, as indeed there are versions of snap, pairs and numerous versions of *Monopoly* that set the gameplay in different contexts.

Many games involve ups and downs, and of course there are winners and losers, an obvious outcome which itself has informed one of the most significant aspects of political and military thinking in the 20th century known as game theory, which uses the language of win–lose, win–win and lose–lose. Yet life is not a game (although there is a *Game of Life*, originally created in 1860 by Milton Bradley, reissued a century later). Games do reflect aspects and dimensions of life and it is not uncommon to hear people using the language of winning and losing metaphorically. Covid has made us all play the game of life differently, blocking progress forward and causing many to slip downhill or get stuck in a corner of the board where escape or emergence does seem to be a matter of luck or good fortune. To be 'in isolation', whether one has the virus or not, was indeed a form of temporary imprisonment from which there was no 'Get out of quarantine free' card.

Although the apostle Paul makes no reference to board games, they would surely have been known to him. In his correspondence with the Corinthian Christians, we see a fondness for athletic analogies. Before the city of Corinth was destroyed by the Romans in 146BC, it was a centre of commerce and sport, hosting the biennial Isthmian Games. When Julius Caesar rebuilt Corinth a century later, the games returned; Corinth was a competitive place. Paul refused to play their game. He argued that the limits of human behaviour and spirituality are set by God; they are not targets to overleap, benchmarks to beat or games to win. Fellow Christians are coworkers, not rivals. If they become so, there is a good chance that personality conflicts arise. This is what happened in Corinth from time to time, causing Paul distress and difficulty.

Paul reminds us, and them, that however like life games are, they are not to be taken too seriously, nor is life to be treated as a game, a competition or a race. Taking part is more important than winning, and faith is not simply a personal effort but a team activity, exercised in fellowship, common purpose, action and cause. There is a place for everyone who competes, whoever has 'fought the good fight... finished the race... kept the faith' (2 Timothy 4:7).

Almighty God, who in Christ calls us into a journey of faith, be with us amid the ups and downs of life, that in all circumstances we may strive towards the goal you set before us and so reach the realm of resurrection life at the end of lives lived in faith, hope and love. Amen

Christmas

38 Christingle oranges

This is the message we have heard from him and proclaim to you, that God is light and in him there is no darkness at all. If we say that we have fellowship with him while we are walking in darkness, we lie and do not do what is true; but if we walk in the light as he himself is in the light, we have fellowship with one another, and the blood of Jesus his Son cleanses us from all sin…

My little children, I am writing these things to you so that you may not sin. But if anyone does sin, we have an advocate with the Father, Jesus Christ the righteous; and he is the atoning sacrifice for our sins, and not for ours only but also for the sins of the whole world…

I am writing you a new commandment that is true in him and in you, because the darkness is passing away and the true light is already shining. Whoever says, 'I am in the light', while hating a brother or sister, is still in the darkness. Whoever loves a brother or sister lives in the light, and in such a person there is no cause for stumbling.

1 JOHN 1:5–7; 2:1–2, 8–10

For many people, Christmas is about children; it is about the birth of a baby, re-enacted by children in nativity plays, celebrated in the name of a sixth-century bishop who saved children, carrying with it a fairy tale about God being born in a manger and a naive hope for peace and goodwill entertained on the day, but not thereafter. The emotions and

sentiments it engenders and promotes are aspirational and worthy of respect, but, once the carols fade and the leftovers are consumed, Christmas goes back in the box with the baubles, to be largely forgotten until resurrected eleven months later.

Memories of Christmas are not forgotten, though; for many the impressions and sights and sounds and smells of the festive season remain in the consciousness, and one of its recurring aspects is to be found in the full sensory experience. Mulled wine, chocolate, Christmas pudding, mince pies, or even the annual perfume present given to a member of the family bring back memories that are powerful and deeply invested with personal associations. Some of these can invoke sorrow or delight, or even both.

The French author Marcel Proust (1871–1922) wrote a series of novels called *The Remembrance of Times Past* (*Á la recherche du temps perdu*), the key theme of which is involuntary memory: the way in which things resurface in our minds unexpectedly. A famous passage describes the moment when the narrator dips a madeleine into his tea. He shudders and his senses are invaded by a pleasurable memory of his childhood when he used to eat such biscuits, and the full memory of people, places and youthful delight comes flooding back, beyond his conscious control. Such experiences happen to us all, when a personal association invades our thoughts and emotions – joyously, painfully, poignantly. Objects, flavours, sensations, even turns of phrase can do this to us. Christmas is a time when this can happen readily, because for so many people it is redolent with childhood memories.

Christmas 2020 hardly happened at all, and Christmas 2021 was also overcast with the shadow of Covid-19. Coronavirus darkness has demolished and damaged successive Christmases. The sounds and smells of Christmas past were withheld, and while parties, family gatherings, carol services and concerts were obviously lacking, the subliminal deprivations were felt on a deeper, perhaps even inaccessible or unconscious level: a level on which unseen damage is done.

Not everyone feels good at Christmas for various reasons, but many do, although few did in 2020. Peace and goodwill for all people means far less if you cannot see those people, and hold, hug, laugh and cry with them.

One of the most powerful examples of the full Christmas sensory experience, carrying adults back to childhood and bringing the next generation to share in the experience, is the Christingle orange. The feel, touch, smell and appearance of an orange with a candle poking out of it, with cocktail sticks emblazoned with sweets or dried fruit stuck into it, is a unique item of sensory spirituality. It stays with us forever and exudes the very odour of Christmas. '*Quelle est cette odeur agreeable*?' asks the French carol ('What is that goodly fragrance?') It is the fragrance of Christmas, wrapped in a red ribbon, reminding us of the presence of Christ, the wounds of Christ and the light of Christ. Every year parents and children flock to churches to collect their orange and renew their acquaintance with the smells and tastes of the season.

I know this from experience. Having been a vicar in the same parish for 17 years, it was always a delight to welcome each Christmas Eve young people who had been coming all their lives. Teenagers and young adults returned annually – perhaps the only day they ever came to church – to sing the carols, see the nativity story and collect their orange, a Christmas ritual. '*This* is Christmas,' they would say. 'It wouldn't be the same without the Christingle.' Singing 'Away in a Manger' with lights dimmed, candles glowing and skewered oranges aloft brings an annual frisson of inner warmth, as all present are touched by a dose of spiritual renewal. Others present know of the hours of preparation cutting oranges, priming sticks with sweets and tying red ribbons around the citrus globes. Preparing Christingles fills the air with a humid orange odour, while cleaning up afterwards involves scraping the floor of candle wax as well as the remains of sweets which have come too close to the flame. We would not have it otherwise, and nor indeed would the Children's Society, who have promoted the Christingle service for many years.

Christingles were first introduced by Bishop Johannes de Watteville in 1747, and now thousands of children receive them each year at services around Christmastide. It all has meaning. Traditionally, the orange represents the world; the candle represents Christ, as light of the world; a red ribbon wrapped around the orange reminds us of the blood of Christ; and dried fruits or sweets on cocktail sticks pushed into the orange represent the fruits of the earth and the four seasons, or perhaps the wounds of Christ.

These elements can also represent faith, hope and love. The sweets attached to sticks represent sweetness in the place of pain – that can be hope for the world. The red ribbon wraps the globe in the love of Christ, love that expressed itself when he died for us on the cross, 'the atoning sacrifice for our sins', 'cleansing us from all sin'. The candle, representing the light of Christ shining in the darkness, is a beacon of inextinguishable faith, for Christ is not just a baby in the manger; he is the light of the world, in whom 'there is no darkness at all'. So perhaps the Christingle is not childlike at all. Symbolic of the true significance of Jesus, the baby in the manger and the man on the cross, it connects the two, held together by a blood red ribbon.

Father God, grant to us your children all over the globe faith, hope and love offered in the birth, death and resurrection of Jesus Christ our Saviour, for in him, we are in the true light. Amen

New Year

39 Gates

'Very truly, I tell you, anyone who does not enter the sheep-fold by the gate but climbs in by another way is a thief and a bandit. The one who enters by the gate is the shepherd of the sheep. The gatekeeper opens the gate for him, and the sheep hear his voice. He calls his own sheep by name and leads them out. When he has brought out all his own, he goes ahead of them, and the sheep follow him because they know his voice. They will not follow a stranger, but they will run from him because they do not know the voice of strangers.' Jesus used this figure of speech with them, but they did not understand what he was saying to them.

So again Jesus said to them, 'Very truly, I tell you, I am the gate for the sheep. All who came before me are thieves and bandits; but the sheep did not listen to them. I am the gate. Whoever enters by me will be saved, and will come in and go out and find pasture. The thief comes only to steal and kill and destroy. I came that they may have life, and have it abundantly.'

JOHN 10:1–10

The sociologist and poet Minnie Louise Haskins (1875–1957) wrote a poem which was used by King George VI in his Christmas message

broadcast in 1939. Entitled 'God Knows', its opening words are well-known:

> And I said to the man who stood at the gate of the year:
> 'Give me a light that I may tread safely into the unknown.'
> And he replied:
> 'Go out into the darkness and put your hand into the Hand of God.
> That shall be to you better than light and safer than a known way.'
> So I went forth, and finding the Hand of God, trod gladly into the
>   night.
> And He led me towards the hills and the breaking of day in the lone
>   East.

The idea that a gate separates past and future is alluring, because a gate, unlike a door, allows us to see beyond the barrier that it is, to glimpse the territory beyond, to expect, to predict, to hope. In Revelation 3:20 Jesus is likened to a door, but here in John's gospel he describes himself not only as the good shepherd, but also as the gate. The metaphors may seem mixed, and it is the good shepherd that is most remembered, but Jesus also describes himself as a gate, and this is because the best kind of shepherd *is* a gate. At night, when wolves prowl, the sheep are herded and hemmed into the sheep pen – a loose structure of branches – and having called them 'home' to huddle together for warmth and safety, the shepherd lies down across the entrance of the sheep pen, literally blocking it overnight. Any intruding predator has to deal with and get past him. In the morning the shepherd rises and 'opens' the 'gate', allowing the sheep to come and go freely. During the dark night he has, literally, saved their lives.

Just as the spiritual connotations of this illustration are clear, its connections to what we have endured during the Covid-19 pandemic are poignant and noticeable. During lockdowns we were penned at home, gates closed, freedom denied for our own safety. This tactic of lockdowns is to prevent access to, and therefore the spread of, the virus. So the gates were closed and people huddled in their homes, at times fearful, stressed, resentful, despairing even.

Through the closed gates of self-isolation, quarantine and lockdown, the future could be glimpsed, but not grasped. We had to wait for metaphorical dawn before any safe release could be contemplated. The difficulty for we whom the psalmist describes as 'the people of his pasture, and the sheep of his hand' (Psalm 95:7) is the same as for the first-century sheep: we might want to roam about and gambol all day and night, but the gatekeeper knows better. He knows what is good for us and has our best interests at heart. He knows it is dangerous and is also willing to take risks accordingly. The first-century human sheep gate is a physical reality which takes on spiritual meaning as it symbolises the protective relationship between God and us. Under Covid-19 the metaphorical gates of our homes became a representation of an attempt to prevent danger to health founded on the wisdom of science.

Yet it is still the Lord who lays himself down, at personal risk, for us. If we say that the technologies and discoveries and efforts of scientists to alleviate Covid-19, prevent its spread and deliver vaccines is in some sense divinely assisted or inspired, for which we thank God, there is still risk for God today. For not everyone recognises that God can be credited with any involvement at all, and given a tendency to place 'science' in opposition to 'religion', it is science that gets praised, science in whom people trust and medicine in which people now put their faith. God no longer gets any recognition as the creator of a world in which human intelligence, imagination and innovation are emergent from the trinitarian concept of creator, saviour and sustainer of everything. When we have vaccines, who needs God? Who needs a gatekeeper when we have freedom to think as we please, do as we please and solve our own problems? Can we not come and go as we see fit?

Many scientists are not so bold as to believe that science negates God, removing divinity from the picture. Vaccines are remarkable innovations and have, to many minds, been a godsend. But they have not solved the problem, only responded to it. Science does not give an alternative account of the world; it enhances all the accounts we have already, including those provided by intelligent religious people. Invariably the standoff between 'science' and 'religion' is caricatured, loaded and acrimonious. Rather, there is room for nuance, compatibility and mutuality, as well as the fascination and wisdom that comes from the interaction of truths from science and religion. Science advances our knowledge and enables us to achieve remarkable things. Faith gives us context, tradition, truth and values. Ideally, they should walk forward hand in hand.

So whether Jesus is lying down to protect the sheep in the first-century field or we are trying to close the gates on Covid-19 in the 21st century, the underlying pastoral needs and protective care are the same. Both are dangerous, self-sacrificial, caring responses to a phenomenon that, being real, has to be handled carefully, practically and safely, but not without risk. We have seen the severity of that risk in the loss of so many health and key workers who tried to keep Covid-19 at bay and paid the ultimate price. Christ the good shepherd laid down his life, not only low as the sheep gate, but high on the cross.

Gates give a vision to a future beyond: we see through them, with hope, but their vista comes at a high price. And to walk through them we need the light of Christ too, a light to tread safely into the unknown and a hand to hold 'better than light and safer than a known way'. For as God opens for us a new gate of hope, we can step through it, as the hymn writer Henry Francis Lyte (1793–1847) put it, 'ransomed, healed, restored, forgiven' in faith and love into a new post-coronavirus dawn.

Heavenly Father, we bring to your feet the tribute of praise and thanksgiving. As you know the feebleness of our frame, by your grace and favour, bless, tend and spare us from all ills, that with angels and all the dwellers in time and space, we may come to dwell with you, the high eternal, everlasting king. Amen

Winter

40 Shoes

Our steps are made firm by the Lord,
   when he delights in our way;
though we stumble, we shall not fall headlong,
   for the Lord holds us by the hand.

I have been young, and now am old,
   yet I have not seen the righteous forsaken
   or their children begging bread.
They are ever giving liberally and lending,
   and their children become a blessing.

Depart from evil, and do good;
   so you shall abide forever.
For the Lord loves justice;
   he will not forsake his faithful ones.

The righteous shall be kept safe forever,
   but the children of the wicked shall be cut off.
The righteous shall inherit the land,
   and live in it forever.

The mouths of the righteous utter wisdom,
   and their tongues speak justice.
The law of their God is in their hearts;
   their steps do not slip.

PSALM 37:23–31

As we venture out through the gate into new pastures, we continue to look back over our shoulders at the pre-pandemic past; and we may feel we need some new shoes. For our old shoes no longer fit. Spiritually and emotionally, we need new shoes, and they are going to be costly. They are going to cost us something of the past, they will be charged with the old ways, former pleasures and ways of life, which, even if we can retrace those steps, will not be the same.

And even if we want to retrace old steps and reclaim parts of our past, we still need new shoes, because the terrain is different. New shoes are not only a costly investment, for the present and the future, but they have to be worn in. As we walk forward in new shoes in a new world, we must wear our shoes in, in faith, hope and love. Whether they are sturdy boots, elegant Oxfords, trendy trainers or high-class heels, the old ones will not do. It is time to change our shoes.

Shoes are not much mentioned in the Bible, although we can assume that there were in fact many pairs worn by biblical characters, taken for granted, barely mentioned. There are famous examples where shoes are removed rather than put on, which underlines their ubiquity. Moses is told to remove his shoes because he finds himself on holy ground before the burning bush (Exodus 3:5; Acts 7:33). This reflects a servant nature, still found in many faiths today, as slaves did not generally wear shoes in Middle Eastern culture. So to remove shoes is to accept servanthood. (The tradition of removing shoes in the presence of God is not so common in colder climates.) Similarly, to untie someone's sandals is an act of humble service, of which even John the Baptist claimed to be unworthy (Luke 3:16) when he met Jesus. Again, the disciples are sent out on mission with no sandals, symbolising not only their servanthood, but their dependence on others. They are told to shake the dust off their feet if they are denied hospitality (Matthew 10:9–14).

This relates to another Middle Eastern tradition, such that on removing shoes when entering a house, one's feet would be washed as a gesture of soothing welcome. When Jesus visits the house of Simon the Pharisee, he is denied this, and when a woman of the city does it for him, using her hair as towel, Jesus rebukes Simon (Luke 7:44–46). The younger son in the parable is given a new pair of sandals on his return from prodigality (Luke 15:22). This is not only a practical issue (no doubt his sandals, if he had any, were wrecked); it also symbolises a new start, a new journey in life, redeemed, reinstated. In a similar way, God says to Ezekiel that forgiveness and renewal are symbolised by new clothes and sandals (Ezekiel 16:10). By contrast, when Ezekiel's wife dies, God tells him to wear his sandals nevertheless; to hide his grief and move on (Ezekiel 24:15–18).

For both Ezekiel and the prodigal son, shoes symbolise a new start, a new path on which to walk. As we walk forward through the gate and away from the Covid pandemic that has hemmed us in for so long, we might wonder what new shoes to wear on that journey. Shoes are an individual choice, and the range of styles, brands, shapes and sizes is staggering. One size does not fit all, for sure, and different kinds of shoe suit different occasions and activities. It is rare to bump into someone wearing the same shoes as yourself, and yet, in general, everyone wears a pair of shoes most of the time. And we have been doing so for a very long time.

The history of the shoe is the history of humankind. Some museums, such as the Bata Shoe Museum in Toronto, Northampton Museum and the V&A, tell the story of the shoe – from early Egyptian sandals to Jimmy Choo's wondrous artworks for the feet. Shoes throughout history have served the same basic function – to protect our feet. But like any practical object, they have also developed an aesthetic history of how they can be made to look good as well as feel good to the wearer. Shoe aficionados tell us that some of the best-looking shoes are in fact very uncomfortable. High heels take some getting used to and, as well as potentially causing pain in other parts of the body, can restrict movement and agility significantly.

Movement was restricted during pandemic lockdowns, but not by our shoes. After lockdowns we have been able to set off into a post-pandemic world, striding into the familiar but unknown. When we do so, are we shod in hiking boots, ready for all weathers, robust in the ruts of mud into which we would otherwise sink? Do we stride forth in the confidence of good soles and lasting hope? Or are we still holding our stilettos in our hands, peering through the gate, wisely cautious of the terrain, aware that if we take one step we will sink sharply into the clay? Or perhaps we wear trainers: flexible shoes for the sport of re-emergence, agile footwear to make us fleet of foot in the face of future fear. Or perhaps we are still in our slippers: the shoes we wore at home for winter lockdowns, when we barely went out of the door of our gated existence. I daresay many people wore out their house slippers during lockdowns. I certainly found that some days I never donned outdoor shoes.

To re-enter a world that was so changed, we needed to be resoled, newly heeled for the future, for ourselves and our relationships. But step through the gate into the future we did, perhaps with a spring in our step, as we strove to walk in the byways of righteousness, in the way of Christ, with God's word as a lamp to our feet and a light on our path of faith.

Journey with us God, in all our ways, that we may walk by faith not sight, stepping forward in hope and trusting in the light of your love, now and always. Amen

41 Plagues and pandemics

He sent his servant Moses,
  and Aaron whom he had chosen.
They performed his signs among them,
  and miracles in the land of Ham.
He sent darkness, and made the land dark;
  they rebelled against his words.
He turned their waters into blood,
  and caused their fish to die.
Their land swarmed with frogs,
  even in the chambers of their kings.
He spoke, and there came swarms of flies,
  and gnats throughout their country.
He gave them hail for rain,
  and lightning that flashed through their land.
He struck their vines and fig trees,
  and shattered the trees of their country.
He spoke, and the locusts came,
  and young locusts without number;
they devoured all the vegetation in their land,
  and ate up the fruit of their ground.
He struck down all the firstborn in their land,
  the first issue of all their strength.

PSALM 105:26–36

Like many communities before and since, the Israelites in Egypt endured hardship, misery, material shortages, mistreatment and restriction of movement. Moses pleaded with Pharaoh to 'let my people go', but it took ten plagues, each more terrible than the last,

to persuade him to relent (Exodus 7:14—12:32). Even then the Egyptians gave chase and were only stopped as Moses and his people crossed the sea, which divided to let them pass (Exodus 14). This is the story of the salvation of ancient Israel, and it is commemorated annually at the festival of the Passover, which it inaugurated. Psalm 105 abbreviates the story for liturgical use and places it within a wider narrative of God's faithfulness to the Israelites. That Jesus was crucified at Passover time reminds us that his death and resurrection can be thought of as a second exodus, as God's people are released from the slavery of sin and led to a new land of resurrection life.

However we understand the plagues of Egypt and Moses' part in bringing about divine threat against Pharaoh, this human story of suffering through pestilence is real to us and to any culture or period of history that has endured widespread, continuous natural disaster or disease. Our recent experience of pandemic resonates with this story, as does so much suffering which we have not personally endured but have seen or read about.

In addition to the biblical plagues, the earliest recorded epidemic was the Plague of Athens in 430BC. Almost a thousand years later came the Justinian Plague of AD541. The 14th-century Black Death, the Great Plague of London in the 1660s and the Spanish influenza pandemic at the end of World War I also spring to mind. Plagues are not a purely biblical phenomenon, nor a solely modern one; they are a fact of life, whatever we call them.

The biblical plagues of Egypt have elicited some scientific explanations by those who seek to relate them to historical events or natural occurrences that may have arisen in ancient Egypt around the time of the exodus. Those who propose a date for these events tend to place them in the 13th or 12th century BC.

The first plague, of the waters turning into blood, has been diagnosed as a bloom of red algae, which not only makes the water appear red, but is poisonous to fish and any that consume them. Airborne parti-cles from the algae can cause breathing difficulties too. Vast collec-tions of frogs are not so rare, and their corpses attract insects. Fleas could transmit the bacteria *Yersinia pestis*, which causes bubonic plague, which manifests itself in boil-like buboes in victims. Or the boils may have been caused by *Staphylococcus aureus*, bacteria com-monly found on skin. Another theory suggests that this plague may have been smallpox, which was also common in ancient Egypt.

The disease which killed the cattle could have been transmitted by insects, such as bluetongue or African horse sickness. Alternatively it might have been rinderpest, which was identified in Egypt 5,000 years ago and which was finally eradicated worldwide in 2011, its last recorded case being in Kenya in 2001. The hail and fire which fol-lowed may have been caused by an eruption of the volcanic island of Santorini in the Aegean Sea. If so, that would have created higher humidity and rainfall, creating an environment in which locusts could thrive and proliferate. Similarly the ensuing darkness could have been a cloud of volcanic ash, or simply a solar eclipse.

The final and most terrible plague, the death of the firstborn, has been traced back to that algal bloom, releasing airborne toxins which could be inhaled or ingested, perhaps having settled on grain in fields or stores. Since it might well have been the firstborn who picked and fetched the grain, they would be most susceptible to these toxins. (See **livescience.com/58638-science-of-the-10-plagues.html**.)

We will never likely know the facts, if any, which underpin the bibli-cal story, but the possible scientific explanations open the poignant possibility that the firstborn of Egypt were slain by airborne particles which caused breathing difficulty, disease and death among those who unwittingly went too close for safety. The Covid-19 pandemic alerted us to the dangers of airborne infection. Facemasks and social distancing helped us a great deal, but these forces of nature are hard to defeat, even in our highly educated, scientific, technological times.

When we view the ten plagues through the lens of a pandemic, we can contemplate scientific explanations for events that have religious significance. Likewise, we may say that there are spiritual dimensions to events or phenomena that appear to be purely scientific or political in the broad sense of the word. The lines dividing the spiritual and the physical, the scientific and the religious are not as sharp as some would like to draw them. The angel of death may have a scientific explanation, and the scientific progress and discovery that has helped us over the years can be thought of, and given thanks for, spiritually too.

All things in heaven and on earth have meaning beyond their surface appearance. The release from slavery that the tenth plague brought about, through the passing over of the angel of death, prefigured the greater redemption wrought in Jesus Christ. By the same token, we thank God for the creation of treatments and vaccines, not simply in terms of our own personal protection, but in respect of the communal and worldwide benefit they can give to all God's people of every race, religion and colour.

Next time you encounter a natural disaster or medical crisis, think not only of all who suffer, but also of the gifts and skills which help humanity endure it. Give thanks to God.

God, you have created all things and will the flourishing of all creation. Where human sin, foolishness or natural disaster shake the world, pour down your compassion on all who suffer or who labour for the relief of others. Console us all with the greater hope you reveal in the ministry and mission of Jesus Christ your Son our Lord. Amen

42 Vaccines

Moses called all the elders of Israel and said to them, 'Go, select lambs for your families, and slaughter the passover lamb. Take a bunch of hyssop, dip it in the blood that is in the basin, and touch the lintel and the two doorposts with the blood in the basin. None of you shall go outside the door of your house until morning. For the Lord will pass through to strike down the Egyptians; when he sees the blood on the lintel and on the two doorposts, the Lord will pass over that door and will not allow the destroyer to enter your houses to strike you down. You shall observe this rite as a perpetual ordinance for you and your children. When you come to the land that the Lord will give you, as he has promised, you shall keep this observance. And when your children ask you, "What do you mean by this observance?" you shall say, "It is the passover sacrifice to the Lord, for he passed over the houses of the Israelites in Egypt, when he struck down the Egyptians but spared our houses." And the people bowed down and worshipped.

The Israelites went and did just as the Lord had commanded Moses and Aaron.

At midnight the Lord struck down all the firstborn in the land of Egypt, from the firstborn of Pharaoh who sat on his throne to the firstborn of the prisoner who was in the dungeon, and all the firstborn of the livestock. Pharaoh arose in the night, he and all his officials and all the Egyptians; and there was a loud cry in Egypt, for there was not a house without someone dead.

EXODUS 12:21–30

The story of the Lord striking down the firstborn of the Egyptians seems cruel. The killing of unblemished lambs, painting their blood on doorposts as a kind of vaccine against death, is hard to swallow. There seems to be double innocence here: the poor lambs and the firstborn animals and children. It would have been a devastating blow, causing widespread grief and financial hardship. Such conditions are not strange to those of us who have lived through the coronavirus pandemic, with its high death toll, wholesale grieving and financially ruinous consequences.

Yet when we look back on the coronavirus pandemic, we cannot downplay the good effect of vaccines. As we recall the first Passover, when the angel of death struck down all but those who had taken steps to protect themselves and their families, we find a resonance with pandemic days. Where there is dangerous disease, avoidance is useful, but not reliable: airborne particles do not know about social distancing or any other human behaviour. We can avoid them as best we can, but we also need protection. In ancient Egypt protection was given by the blood of a lamb or goat, an uninfected, unblemished beast, whose sacrifice vaccinated the people of God from death visited upon them by an external force.

Vaccines were developed with the help of cows, rather than sheep or goats. The word itself comes from the Latin word *vacca*, for cow. In 1796 Edward Jenner (1749–1823) successfully immunised an eight-year-old boy against smallpox with infected fluid from a milkmaid who had cowpox. While he gets the credit for this, he was not the first to try it. An earlier, related technique known as variolation was used in China in the tenth century, by which scratches would be made in the skin and infected matter brought into contact with it. The word 'inoculation' comes from the idea of grafting one plant into another (a metaphor used by Paul in Romans 11:17–24). This approach to the virulent smallpox was observed not only in China but also Turkey and was tried on prisoners in Newgate Prison, London, in the mid-18th century. At that point, the word 'inoculation' referred only to variolation, and smallpox immunisation continued to be called variolation, whereas Jenner's approach using cowpox to give immunity to small-pox became known as 'vaccination'. Variolation is the oldest method, and relates solely to smallpox inoculation (*variolae* is smallpox).

The basic idea is that a small infection would lead to protection against greater, more dangerous infection. In 1861 the French scientist Louis Pasteur suggested that the term 'vaccination' be extended to cover a wide range of techniques. In the 21st century any injection of an immunity-producing solution into the body is known as a vaccination, but it was not always the case. Vaccination is administered through the needle, injected into muscle tissue. Immunisation is the word given to the whole process, and it is the process, not the vaccination itself, by which immunity is generated. Some immunisations – such as against Covid-19 or hepatitis – involve more than one separate vaccination to complete the process.

Immunisation has a wider remit, including the techniques of introducing pre-made antibodies into a patient. Antibodies fight antigens and are generally created by the body in response to the introduction of alien antigens. Usually immunisation stimulates this production of antibodies by provoking them with a small quantity of antigens. Thus the body 'learns' to fight them, 'remembers' them and any further 'attack' is dealt with, often without symptoms at all. In some forms of immunisation, pre-made antibodies are directly introduced into the body, rather than using the immune system to create them naturally.

While in modern parlance, the terms 'vaccination' and 'immunisation' (and sometimes also 'inoculation') are often used interchangeably, no doubt to the annoyance of pedants and microbiologists, the differences between these approaches to preventing infection have spiritual resonance.

Protected by a radical intervention that was prescribed externally but administered by themselves, the Israelites can be thought of as receiving an initial vaccine against judgement and destruction – that is, the blood on the doorposts. God gave them a kind of first jab against ill effects, a preventative prescription to ward off danger. Daubing the doorposts was a treatment, the administration of which was the difference between life and death.

But it was also more than that. The various Covid-19 vaccines work in subtly different biological ways, but the ultimate effect of all of them is to 'teach' the body to defend itself against the virus. In the same way, at that first Passover, God was teaching the Israelites what to do to obtain inner protection from a localised epidemic which would immediately cause widespread suffering. History tells us the Jewish people remained grateful for this intervention for centuries and still celebrate their redemption from slavery to this day.

So we can also think of that first Passover as the first step in a process of immunisation. It was a one-off event which marked the beginning of a process of protection, national identity and spiritual awakening as they learned to love God, live well and defend themselves against evil. Unfortunately, the Old Testament is a catalogue of how this process faltered and ultimately failed, as they fell away from or rebelled against God repeatedly. Only in the coming of the Messiah would full immunity, full protection against judgement and full freedom from the slavery of sin be secured in the hope and promise of resurrection life for all God's creation.

When you recall the vaccinations you have had, reflect on the greater immunity to the impact of sin God has given us in Jesus Christ.

Christ our Saviour, who by your holy cross has saved and immunised the world against sin, prick our consciences with self-awareness of our human weakness, made healthy by the assurance of our ultimate hope in you. Amen

43 Second jab

Therefore, just as sin came into the world through one man, and death came through sin, and so death spread to all because all have sinned – sin was indeed in the world before the law, but sin is not reckoned when there is no law. Yet death exercised dominion from Adam to Moses, even over those whose sins were not like the transgression of Adam, who is a type of the one who was to come.

But the free gift is not like the trespass. For if the many died through the one man's trespass, much more surely have the grace of God and the free gift in the grace of the one man, Jesus Christ, abounded for the many. And the free gift is not like the effect of the one man's sin. For the judgement following one trespass brought condemnation, but the free gift following many trespasses brings justification. If, because of the one man's trespass, death exercised dominion through that one, much more surely will those who receive the abundance of grace and the free gift of righteousness exercise dominion in life through the one man, Jesus Christ.

Therefore just as one man's trespass led to condemnation for all, so one man's act of righteousness leads to justification and life for all. For just as by the one man's disobedience the many were made sinners, so by the one man's obedience the many will be made righteous.

ROMANS 5:12–19

Vaccination is an event and immunisation is a process. A vaccination programme seeks to build up a community's immunity by artificial means, albeit using natural ingredients derived from the virus or

bacteria itself. The process can involve more than one 'jab' for the immunity to be complete. Between each jab – of Covid vaccine injections, for example – there is some protection, but there is still vulnerability and danger. Back in 2021 we were often reminded that one jab was not sufficient.

Furthermore, for an immunisation programme to be effective, almost everyone needs to participate to create 'herd immunity'. Herd immunity can be achieved naturally, through death; that is, through a process not dissimilar to natural selection whereby those who can survive a disease do so, and those who cannot, do not. Eventually only survivors will be left, and they will be immune through either having overcome the disease, natural immunity or simply having the good fortune not to have been exposed to it. This approach seems harsh (and can overwhelm health services) and was deliberately rejected by many western governments who had sufficient resources to prevent it. In some countries, however, where there was no treatment, cure or vaccination programme, many thousands died, unaided by modern science, financial support or compassionate leadership.

Vaccinations and the immunity they yield are a great gift. The principles underlying the process are natural and God-given. The technology is developed by humans, but it is ultimately grounded in the innate human quest for knowledge and our capacity for wisdom and intelligence. These two are part of the natural order of things and come from God, the creator of all things. They are part of the goodness of God and are revealed as a beneficial aspect of human existence and flourishing. They can be used for great kindness, mutual care, growth and fullness of life.

We have capacity for goodness, as was evident in spades during the lockdowns. Churches, community groups and individuals showed sacrificial kindness to friends and strangers alike. For many months key workers laboured relentlessly in the valley of death. Covid-19 brought out the best in so many. Yet humanity is not good. Even our best is not good enough, and we have known this since the fall of Adam.

There are many ways to read and interpret the story of the fall, which is rich in symbolism, meaning and metaphor as well as outlining the basic truth which none can doubt: that human beings are flawed, sinful, selfish; we damage others and are damaged ourselves. The story of Adam and Eve succumbing in the garden of Eden adds colour and power to the deep and dangerous truth of weakness and imperfection. The ancient and powerful narrative of serpent and fruit speaks to us of the fundamental truth that, though creatures of God, we are in need of redemption.

There is also the idea, given to us by the apostle Paul, that Christ is like a second Adam, coming to fight against sin: 'a second Adam' who 'to the fight and to the rescue came'. That phrase comes from the wonderful hymn 'Praise to the holiest in the height' by John Henry Newman (1801–90), which formed part of his epic poem *The Dream of Gerontius*. He continues the idea:

> *O wisest love, that flesh and blood*
> *which did in Adam fail,*
> *should strive afresh against the foe,*
> *should strive and should prevail.*

Jesus, the second Adam, puts right what was, and still is, wrong with Adam – and Adam means you and me. Christ has won that battle, in the garden of Gethsemane secretly and on the cross on high, where he willingly went to suffer and to die. Paul is clear that although we are saved by Christ we are still born of Adam.

In creation, God did not give humanity full immunity from sin, and we were soon infected with it (as characterised by the wily serpent's temptation of Eve and Adam). A process of immunisation was needed, and the Old Testament testifies to a long period of frailty, weakness and failure among God's people. In the (first) coming of the Messiah, Jesus Christ, God administers a jab of redemption, a powerful dose to free us from the slavery of sin. Paul calls Jesus the second Adam because he undoes the primary infection of sin.

This first vaccination against sin, as we might put it, is a huge dose of grace. Injected into the muscles of humanity, it gives strength and succour against sin, and a blessed assurance of future hope and redemption. The second coming, the second jab, will complete the process of immunisation from human sin and will alleviate creation's continued groaning for redemption (Romans 8:18–23).

Currently we live in the period that some theologians call the 'middle time', the 'now and not yet', a period of graceful space and time in which we have had the first jab and yet await the second to complete the process. This means we live in a world beset with sin, but in which we can also see great goodness, in humanity and nature. Ultimate perfection is yet to come, but we have seen enough to glimpse its power and grace.

Both physical and spiritual vaccinations are all about grace. A jab in the arm is witness to the grace of God revealed in human endeavour, wisdom and skill, ministered among ourselves to his glory. Spiritual vaccination comes through the incarnation of Jesus Christ, who redeemed the world by the piercing of his own hands, feet and side. In this, he gave sufficient protection and helped us recognise, even begin to build, immunity from the eternally deadly impact of sin. It is this grace in which we rejoice and which gives us ultimate healing and hope. If you have been vaccinated, reflect on the grace it presents to your body and represents in your heart.

Father God, you have blessed us with immunity from sin. By the ongoing grace of the Holy Spirit dwelling in our hearts, protect and build us up in loving, merciful behaviour that reflects the ultimate victory over sin and death won by your Son, our Lord Jesus Christ. Amen

44 Masks

> Moses came down from Mount Sinai. As he came down from
> the mountain with the two tablets of the covenant in his hand,
> Moses did not know that the skin of his face shone because
> he had been talking with God. When Aaron and all the Isra-
> elites saw Moses, the skin of his face was shining, and they
> were afraid to come near him. But Moses called to them; and
> Aaron and all the leaders of the congregation returned to him,
> and Moses spoke with them. Afterward all the Israelites came
> near, and he gave them in commandment all that the Lord had
> spoken with him on Mount Sinai. When Moses had finished
> speaking with them, he put a veil on his face; but whenever
> Moses went in before the Lord to speak with him, he would
> take the veil off, until he came out; and when he came out,
> and told the Israelites what he had been commanded, the
> Israelites would see the face of Moses, that the skin of his face
> was shining; and Moses would put the veil on his face again,
> until he went in to speak with him.
>
> EXODUS 34:29–35

Before the pandemic began, most people in western countries
thought it rather odd to wear a face mask, associating it with a Far
Eastern response to severe pollution. I myself had only ever really
worn one in 2008 when I led a parish pilgrimage to China and we were
advised to wear them in Beijing because of the poor air quality. It was
a strange experience, being in Tiananmen Square, recalling the tragic
events of June 1989 when the Chinese government violently crushed
peaceful protests. Yet there we were in that huge outdoor space, protecting ourselves from a very different kind of pollution. We never

imagined that twelve years later we would be wearing these masks every day, or at least on the rare occasions we left home.

The principle and practice of covering one's face has a convoluted and controversial history. People do it for different reasons – cultural, religious, sinister and practical. Criminals cover their faces so they cannot be recognised. Medics wear surgical masks to prevent infection and contamination. Face coverings disguise beauty from prying eyes, or disfigurement from judgemental eyes. Brides traditionally wear veils to preserve modesty, although it is a matter of law that the veil must be removed before the vows so that the husband can see whom he is marrying. (This takes us back to Jacob and Rachel and Leah, the latter of whom we assume was married in a veil, in order to deceive Jacob into marrying the 'wrong' sister – Genesis 29:15–30.)

The oldest extant masks are over 9,000 years old and are in museums in Paris and Jerusalem. These ancient masks often had ritualistic functions, and in other ancient cultures masks were used in theatrical, dramatic or playful contexts. Masks enable a wearer to be someone else, disguising the true persona and presenting a false, imaginary or representative face to onlookers. In a sense, therefore, the history of masks carries us back deep into cultural and psychological understandings of what it is to be human.

During the coronavirus pandemic, wearing a mask sent a message – 'I'm protecting myself and others'. Conversely, any refusal or reticence to wear a mask also begged interpretation. Some people were exempt from covering their faces for various medical reasons, but as the pandemic developed through 2020, mandatory face coverings became almost universally accepted as a valuable precaution against airborne infection. Many people still wear them for this reason. Mask-wearing went from being a niche activity to mainstream behaviour, thanks to Covid-19, legislation and explanation.

We cannot know exactly what Moses wore to protect his face, or why. Moses seems to be exercising a priestly function in this story – acting as an intermediary between God and the people – and it was not unusual for priests in ancient cultures to wear masks. Sometimes the mask represented the deity or an aspect of divine power. Some commentators draw on this anthropology to suggest that Moses wore a mask with horns; Michelangelo's sculpture of Moses in the Church of St Peter in Vincoli in Rome depicts him in this way. On the other hand, the idea that Moses' mask had horns comes from a mistranslation of the Hebrew in the Vulgate – the Latin translation of the Bible by St Jerome in the fourth century.

It is thought that Israelite priests wore face coverings when entering the holy sanctuary to be veiled in the presence of – and to some extent be protected from – the glory of God. Here it is the other way around: Moses did not wear the mask when in God's presence, but rather put it on when in the less glorious presence of the people, to protect them from seeing the effect of glory of God. That is, Moses wore the mask for their sake, not his own. As in pandemic times, the mask offers more protection to others than oneself.

For Christians the glory of God is revealed in Jesus Christ. As Paul put it: 'God… has shone in our hearts to give the light of the knowledge of the glory of God in the face of Jesus Christ' (2 Corinthians 4:6). When Jesus was transfigured on the mountain, his 'face shone like the sun' (Matthew 17:2) and the connection with Moses' veiled face is deliberate in both passages. Whatever glory Moses experienced is enhanced permanently in Jesus' face. Jesus, God incarnate, human and divine, reflects a unity such that we can see the face of Jesus Christ in all humanity, made as we are in the image of God. To see others, to help others, to serve others and to love others is to see, help, serve and love God.

Wearing a face mask to protect others from infection is a Christlike gesture and Christian action. Doing so is a humble, perhaps even mildly humiliating, act of service and love which puts others first, while concealing the glorious servanthood of doing so; could we but see it, there would be a glow of mutual care and compassion inspired by the call of Christ to love our neighbours as ourselves without making a fuss about it.

Next time you wear a mask, or see others doing so, remember that this simple act is not so much self-centred, but a true expression of good neighbourly faith and compassionate action.

Father God, whose loving gaze is turned towards your world in the face of Jesus Christ, illuminate our lives with the glow of your compassion, so that whether our faces are masked or not, we may reflect your loving mercy. Amen

45 Personal protective equipment

Be strong in the Lord and in the strength of his power. Put on the whole armour of God, so that you may be able to stand against the wiles of the devil. For our struggle is not against enemies of blood and flesh, but against the rulers, against the authorities, against the cosmic powers of this present darkness, against the spiritual forces of evil in the heavenly places. Therefore take up the whole armour of God, so that you may be able to withstand on that evil day, and having done everything, to stand firm. Stand therefore, and fasten the belt of truth around your waist, and put on the breastplate of righteousness. As shoes for your feet put on whatever will make you ready to proclaim the gospel of peace. With all of these, take the shield of faith, with which you will be able to quench all the flaming arrows of the evil one. Take the helmet of salvation, and the sword of the Spirit, which is the word of God.

EPHESIANS 6:10–17

The Covid-19 pandemic saw the reintroduction of body armour. Previously it was only riot police, security guards, motorcyclists and soldiers who wore it, and even then not systematically or constantly. Armour is protective, but it is uncomfortable, heavy and restricts movement. David is famously able to kill Goliath because he is fleet of foot and not weighed down by the heavy armour which Saul tries to make him wear (1 Samuel 17).

More recently, body armour has taken on a new name – personal protective equipment. PPE is medical armour, and it is not optional

when there is a virus on the attack. It is cumbersome, restrictive and uncomfortable. Many a doctor, nurse or other key worker knows this first hand and has endured plasticated shielding for a long time now. Hitherto it was reserved for intensive care units and only rarely worn by the wider public, yet in March 2020 it entered the vocabulary and cultural fabric of the nation, as its necessity, and shortage, became public knowledge.

Those in the frontline of the battle against the coronavirus tooled up in blue fatigues and fought the invading virus. A metaphorical war was declared against a deadly enemy, and those engaged in medical conflict needed to be protected. Some were not, and many suffered and died – nurses, doctors, care home staff, transport workers alike. We mourn them still: those who fell in action, succumbing to the disease that harmed those they tried to help. Among a nation of people whom barely remember wartime, this was the next worst thing.

Over the centuries, armour has been made of a variety of strong substances – leather, wood, metal, Kevlar – and the making of armour has driven technological development. The need to protect oneself from enemies has never been absent. The apostle Paul, who had a knack of relating his teaching of the faith to familiar objects, used the concept of armour spiritually in this famous passage, in which he turns something which speaks of the arrogance and violence of humanity into something spiritually empowering. He introduces us to the armour of God: spiritual armour against an unseen but pervasive force which was understood in Paul's time to undermine, destroy and weaken the spirit, allowing in sin, demonic influence and ultimately, perhaps, mental illness and even death. In writing to the pagan converts in Ephesus, Paul used words that resonate with the modern need of medical PPE.

Like the forces that Paul's spiritual armour protects against, viruses are unseen, pervasive and dangerous, even deadly. Over the years, the language of viral infection has extended to computer technology – the way in which a computer virus infects a network and replicates itself is to some extent analogous to what real viruses do. Viruses are not cellular and are not considered to be living organisms – they rely on the cellular machinery of the host.

With all these metaphors flying around, perhaps we can think of sin as a kind of a virus. Sin is in the air, it is all around us, and it is easy to be infected by it: we all *are* infected by it. Sin is not a thing in itself, it needs a host in which to thrive and replicate. Sin cannot sit on a bench and mind its own business. Sin is harmless if it is not in a person. But when we catch it – as we all have done – it latches on, separates us from God and grows within us. We cough and sneeze sin, and it does damage to ourselves and others. It can infect others.

We never achieve immunity to sin, although we can try to protect ourselves by donning the armour of God. Just as we can attempt to treat a virus, we can try to treat sin. We may never get rid of it – it is not living nor non-living – but we can learn to live with it, can learn to live in a world separated from God by sin and can take precautions against it. We treat sinful behaviour with the mercy of God, administered where there is repentance. We take precautions against catching more sin by donning the armour of God: the belt of truth; the breastplate of righteousness; shoes of readiness to proclaim the gospel; the shield of faith; the helmet of salvation; and the sword of the Spirit.

These are Paul's weapons and armour for the fight against sin and evil. In modern language, we might say these are the pills, the precautions and the treatment we should take. How might a modern Ephesian be counselled? Might they be advised to 'take the tablet of truth, the medicine of righteousness, the hand gel of faith to quench the onslaught of nasty bugs, the face mask of salvation and the vaccine of the Spirit, which is the word of God, to fend off all assaults of body and soul'?

While this modern equivalent may make us smile, it is serious. Covid was and still is a serious matter. And so is sin. Both need to be pro-tected against, handled with care, precautioned, managed, cleansed and defeated. And in respect of both, we put our trust in reason and faith. We trust in science and God.

So, whether in body, mind or spirit, as Paul puts it: 'Put on the armour of God, and keep alert and always persevere in supplication for all the saints.' When you see someone wearing PPE, or do so yourself, remember the fight against Covid and all who wore their armour with determination, courage and love, and remember the armour of God that protects us from sin and death.

Christ, protect me today against poison, against burning, against drowning, against wound, that I may receive abundant reward. Salvation is the Lord's. Salvation is Christ's. May your salvation, Lord, be always with us! Amen

Adapted from the ninth-century *St Patrick's Breastplate*.

Lent

46 Lenten season

Yet even now, says the Lord,
    return to me with all your heart,
with fasting, with weeping, and with mourning;
    rend your hearts and not your clothing.
Return to the Lord, your God,
    for he is gracious and merciful,
slow to anger, and abounding in steadfast love,
    and relents from punishing.
Who knows whether he will not turn and relent,
    and leave a blessing behind him,
a grain-offering and a drink-offering
    for the Lord, your God?

Blow the trumpet in Zion;
    sanctify a fast;
call a solemn assembly;
    gather the people.
Sanctify the congregation;
    assemble the aged;
gather the children,
    even infants at the breast.
Let the bridegroom leave his room,
    and the bride her canopy.

> Between the vestibule and the altar
>   let the priests, the ministers of the Lord, weep.
> Let them say, 'Spare your people, O Lord,
>   and do not make your heritage a mockery,
>   a byword among the nations.
> Why should it be said among the peoples,
>   "Where is their God?"'

JOEL 2:12–17

To many people the pandemic felt like a very long Lent. It was a time of privation as some of the pleasures of life were denied or restricted. Initially, after a period of panic-buying, supermarket shelves were laid bare as supply chains broke. Confined to homes, personal relationships were affected, particularly where loved ones were living under different roofs and so were kept apart, at least until 'bubbles' became permitted. Social activity was banned. Easter 2020 did not feel much like Easter as the freedoms of the Paschal Dawn, celebrated away from churches, made us feel that Lent had hardly ended.

Lent 2021 was similarly strange, still affected by lockdown restrictions of various kinds. In 2022 Lent and Holy Week services returned to something like normal, although some people were still reticent to attend larger scale services. While the Russian invasion of Ukraine had pushed Covid off the front pages and the UK government had ended all restrictions, this did not mean it had gone away. Infection rates were still high. We were beginning to learn to live with the coronavirus.

This interruption of our lives for two years – two Lents, two Easters, two Christmases – may have caused us to forget what Lent is. It is good to remind ourselves as we enter another Lent, which comes upon us – as all Lents do – as those who have lived through another year in which the world, and we, have changed. But Lent has not changed. Lent is still the annual season of penitence, the commencement of which is marked by Ash Wednesday. It is preceded by Shrove Tuesday, when it was traditional to consume any luxurious food before the season of self-reflection and self-denial commences.

It does so with an Ash Wednesday service at which ashes are imposed on the forehead, marking the sign of the cross to remind us that 'from dust we came and to dust we shall return' and to 'turn away from sin and be faithful to Christ'.

Lent can be observed in various ways. Benedict recommended daily reading. Many still do that, reading a Lent book: some excellent ones are published each year specifically for this purpose. Others give something up, a worthy discipline, so long as it is something that is done sacrificially and is not trivial. This is fasting, and it carries back to the public acts of fasting to which the prophet Joel refers when entreating the Israelites to 'return to the Lord'. Similarly, one can take something on for Lent, such as some voluntary work, charitable giving or a new routine of prayer or care.

Lent is also a period for personal reflection and prayer – about our sinfulness, our need of mercy and our mortality – and for focusing on the upcoming days of Jesus' passion and resurrection. This Lent, perhaps we might reflect on the 'seven Rs of Lent', as I call them: regret, repentance, recognition, resolution, reconciliation, renewal and resurrection. These seven Rs take us on a journey from our own fallen nature to the cross and beyond. They bear us through faith to hope and love.

Regret is what makes us sigh: the things we look back on in our lives and realise that we did not handle them well, made mistakes, upset others and got it wrong. No one is perfect; we know this, and God knows it. The first stepping stone of Lent is to realise this and be aware of our own regrets, for ourselves and others. We can also regret the things we didn't say or do, especially when it comes to those whom we love and perhaps even see no longer. Hold your regrets before God in sorrowful prayer.

If regret is what makes us sigh, *repentance* is what makes us cry. This second R of our Lenten journey brings us to our knees, sometimes in shame or deep sorrow for the damage we have done to others and to ourselves. It is shameful to hurt others, and it is our shame that leads us to humbly bow before God, assured of forgiveness in Christ in a genuine spirit of desire to wipe the slate clean.

The *recognition* that we are sinners, in need of God's mercy and redemption is an important Lenten one. For if we can recognise ourselves as imperfect and see our own damaged selves in the ways we interact with others, we are, by the grace of God, on the pathway to hope and healing. Lent is also a time to recognise the face and grace of God in others around us, even in those we distrust or despise.

If regret is what makes us sigh and repentance is what makes us cry, *resolution* is what make us try. Having recognised and repented of our failings and foibles, we resolve to do better, to be better and to love others even if they do not love us. Lent is a good time to make resolutions which will benefit not only our physical and mental well-being, but also our spiritual health. So resolution follows regret, repentance and recognition and leads us forward on the journey towards Easter.

The fifth R of Lent is *reconciliation*. It is not easy, having regretted, repented and resolved, to seek reconciliation with anyone whom we have offended, upset or harmed. Yet this is Christ's call, to be reconciled with our brothers and sisters. It is a call for the world to heed. At a personal, local and national level, reconciliation is a call to better living, well-being, security and hope. To be reconciled is to open a doorway to a future of light and love.

If reconciliation opens a doorway to the future, then *renewal*, the sixth R of Lent, is to walk through it in faith, hope and love. As we turn our focus to Christ's suffering on the cross, we are reminded that it is he who is that door, he who invites us through it with arms opened wide in an embrace that speaks not only of love and sacrifice, but of welcome into a kingdom of new-found faith, eternal hope and redeeming love.

All of which points us to the seventh R: *resurrection*.

Merciful God, give us grace to keep a holy Lent, to walk in the way of the cross and follow in the steps of our Lord Jesus Christ, who was tempted as we are, suffered and died but rose again to save and restore us, your damaged and broken people. Amen

47 Covid tests

Jesus replied, 'A man was going down from Jerusalem to Jeri-cho, and fell into the hands of robbers, who stripped him, beat him, and went away, leaving him half dead. Now by chance a priest was going down that road; and when he saw him, he passed by on the other side. So likewise a Levite, when he came to the place and saw him, passed by on the other side. But a Samaritan while travelling came near him; and when he saw him, he was moved with pity. He went to him and band-aged his wounds, having poured oil and wine on them. Then he put him on his own animal, brought him to an inn, and took care of him. The next day he took out two denarii, gave them to the innkeeper, and said, 'Take care of him; and when I come back, I will repay you whatever more you spend.' Which of these three, do you think, was a neighbour to the man who fell into the hands of the robbers?' [The lawyer] said, 'The one who showed him mercy.' Jesus said to him, 'Go and do likewise.'

LUKE 10:30–37

Lent is a testing time, when we 'test' or challenge ourselves, under God, in self-denial, restraint and self-discipline. We might take on charitable acts, devotional reading or some form of abstinence. Lent lasts 46 days, from Ash Wednesday to Easter Day, and every year we embark upon it differently, because we are different: we have changed in the preceding year. We have aged, we have loved and lost and learnt and left part of ourselves in the past. We also look to the future in Lent: in immediate anticipation of Easter, to the months and years beyond, and ultimately to eternal, resurrection life. Every year we do this and each year it is the same yet also different.

The first lockdowns began in March 2020, around Mothering Sunday – the centrepiece of Lent. Lent was altered and Easter cancelled in church, with celebrations taking place around dining tables on Zoom. The archbishop of Canterbury conducted an Easter service from his kitchen table, and I lit the paschal candle in my dining room. The parish drama group recorded a dramatised version of the passion and resurrection scenes, and I delivered palm crosses through letterboxes around the parish.

It was my last Easter in the parish after 17 years as vicar. A month later we moved out without ceremony, still during lockdown. My daughter's GCSEs were cancelled, and there was no farewell do or service. It was a testing time, although very many others really suffered and struggled, in those days and subsequently. We can remind ourselves again and again, not only of the psychological, physical and emotional strain of those times on victims and their families, but also of the extremely testing time that key workers had of it. We owe them a huge debt of gratitude.

Healthcare services not only embarked on treatment, prevention and the herculean effort to produce and distribute vaccines, they also produced the wherewithal for mass testing. Having moved to Rochester Cathedral during lockdown, by November we had converted our 13th-century crypt into an asymptomatic testing centre. It was the least we could do, and it was humbling to welcome thousands of people from North Kent who were key workers, all helping and trying to protect others. It was not long afterwards that the 'Kent variant' of Covid-19 was so named: we found ourselves in the midst of a pandemic hotspot and local medical services were nearly overwhelmed as Christmas 2020 came and went.

Those days passed, and we entered new phases of the pandemic. Vaccines were introduced and the ability to offer mass testing not only to anyone with symptoms, but also to those without them, increased, such that by the middle of 2021, lateral flow testing kits were freely available. The pandemic period also became a testing time of another, better sort. For just as it was often said that, like Moses, we wear masks for the benefit of our neighbours (see 'Masks', page 181), so too are Covid tests a reassurance not only for ourselves but for those with whom we work, play and live. Covid tests, like masks, gave us an opportunity to care *about* others, while key workers cared *for* them.

The idea that I or you could be a danger to someone else without being aware of it is a strange one, which before Covid would not really have occurred to us. Worse still is the idea that I might be unknowingly infected with a disease that could kill you. When the priest and the Levite in the story of the good Samaritan pass by the man left for dead, one of their excuses might have been that, whether he be alive or dead, they should not go near him for fear of infection or ritual uncleanliness.

The fear that someone could infect you with something deadly can be as paralysing as the fear of being mugged. The Australian government threatened to make deliberately infecting someone with Covid a crime potentially punishable with a life sentence. For Covid-19 is like an unseen, malicious brigand who attacks unawares, silently, stealing health and life as well as wealth. Many feel robbed by the virus in various ways: of loved ones, livelihood, mental health, freedom. Others are suffering the effects of 'long Covid', such that even after having been cared for, there are ongoing costs to both wallet and well-being. Notice that the Samaritan stranger provides not only for the present needs of the victim, but for his future needs, underwriting the cost of his care.

However we look back over the Covid-19 period, it is not over and, even as life returns to 'normal', there are many whose lives have been changed forever, not least by loss and future disadvantage. They are our neighbours and we theirs. So we seek God's mercy not only for them, but also for ourselves as we try to be agents of God's grace where there is damage and distress for those waylaid by the troubles and trials of our times.

God, give us grace to be your Samaritans, even when tested. As you have no hands on earth but ours, empower your people with goodness, kindness and compassion, that we may bear witness to your love for all revealed in Jesus Christ our Lord. Amen

48 Quarantine

The person who has the leprous disease shall wear torn clothes and let the hair of his head be dishevelled; and he shall cover his upper lip and cry out, 'Unclean, unclean.' He shall remain unclean as long as he has the disease; he is unclean. He shall live alone; his dwelling shall be outside the camp.

Concerning clothing: when a leprous disease appears in it, in woollen or linen cloth… if the disease shows greenish or reddish in the garment, whether in warp or woof or in skin or in anything made of skin, it is a leprous disease and shall be shown to the priest. The priest shall examine the disease, and put the diseased article aside for seven days. He shall examine the disease on the seventh day. If the disease has spread in the cloth, in warp or woof, or in the skin, whatever be the use of the skin, this is a spreading leprous disease; it is unclean. He shall burn the clothing…

If … the disease has not spread in the clothing … the priest shall command them to wash the article in which the disease appears, and he shall put it aside for seven days more… If the diseased spot has not changed colour, though the disease has not spread, it is unclean; you shall burn it in fire…

If… the disease has abated after it is washed, he shall tear the spot out of the cloth… If it appears again… it is spreading; you shall burn with fire that in which the disease appears. But the cloth, warp or woof, or anything of skin from which the disease disappears when you have washed it, shall then be washed a second time, and it shall be clean.

LEVITICUS 13:45–59

Quarantine reminds us of Lent, a 40-day period of withdrawal, isolation, self-denial and repentance. One of the first examples of quarantine dates from 1377 in Ragusa, a former Venetian colony (now Dubrovnik). It lasted 30 days and was called the *trentino*, but other places, mostly ports, who adopted the idea varied the length to prevent the spread of plague. In Marseilles in 1383, 40 days were insisted upon, to mirror Lent and its biblical 40 days, and the Venetians likewise extended their regulations and renamed it *quarantine* in 1448. From 1423 they had allocated one of their islands for the isolation of incoming seafarers and ships – calling it Lazaretto (after Lazarus, the beggar infested with sores in Luke 16:20). Over 1,500 plague victims were buried there between the 15th and 17th centuries. As it was reckoned that the average period from infection to death from bubonic plague was 37 days, a period of 40 days, as well as being biblical, was eminently sensible.

This takes us back to the second great pandemic, which is usually dated from the beginnings of the Black Death in 1347. There have been two other periods of great plague in recorded history, the first of which is the plague that ravished Europe between the sixth and eighth centuries, which began with the Plague of Justinian in AD541. The most recent plague pandemic is usually dated from the Indian and Chinese pandemics of 1894–1922, and to some extent is still ongoing. Covid-19 is not part of these (it is not a plague strictly speaking), although much of what we have learned about isolation and quarantine is applicable.

Study of the history of pandemics worldwide reveals that most of what we have learnt and developed about public health over the centuries has been formulated on the anvil of the first two global pandemics over the last two millennia, particularly in the first decades of the Black Death. History has much to teach us in dealing with major infectious diseases, and the reactions of the public to restrictions and quarantining is not new or unique to the 21st century. The history of plague in Europe is the history of disease, mass infection, government intervention and control (or lack of it), reaction and resentment and resistance, as well as frustration and public outcry, alongside fear, despair and financial ruin.

History also shows us that any policies put in place by the authorities will be criticised by those who have varying opinions on what is fundamentally a matter of science. As Professor Paul Slack puts it in *Plague: A very short introduction* (OUP, 2021): 'Plague policies and the notions of public health which they embodied were at root political constructs.' There have been, and probably always will be, those who refuse to believe what politicians or medics say, preferring conspiracy theories or alternative sources of information, founded on innate scepticism, religious or political belief, or personal logic. It was ever thus. As the plague in London waned in 1666, partly due to effective quarantine measures, arguments raged and confidence in the authorities plummeted.

Ironically, even for those who adhere to strict religious prohibitions on listening to secular authorities or medical wisdom learned over centuries, the Enlightenment culture since the 17th century not only promoted freedom of information and thought, but had an innate hostility to absolute power exercised by politicians. Those who rebelled against Covid-19 restrictions stand in a long tradition which blends knowledge, arrogance, freedom and self-determination, as well as self-interest in a complex web, which, it has to be said, the media delight in tangling. Which is to say that the ability to criticise or disagree is dependent on the attitudes of an enlightened culture that specifically tolerates such criticism.

Plagues and viruses are not sentient, tolerant or even controllable; rather it is the people who must be engaged with, whether via explanation, persuasion, coercion or restriction. Enforced quarantine is a last resort, but history teaches us it is effective and it serves a greater good. Biblical history teaches us it was also a first resort, introduced into ancient law and implemented swiftly. Lepers were to live 'outside the camp' and their belongings carefully tested and destroyed if necessary. It may seem severe, and even Moses objected when Miriam became leprous (Numbers 12:10–16). King Uzziah was leprous and so lived in a separate house and was excluded from worshipping in God's house (2 Chronicles 26:21).

Plague and disease control from Moses onwards has depended on quarantine. In the absence of cures, infection must be contained, which means containing those who carry it. One of the great paradoxes of life over the past thousand years or so is that we know this, yet resist it. Ancient Jewish beliefs held that disease, and especially leprosy or mass infection, was judgemental punishment from God, so the privations of quarantine were moral and spiritual as well as practical. We need all three to hold the concept of quarantine together: not only does it work practically, but it is also the right thing to do morally, because it protects others, and it is a spiritual discipline to submit to the authority of others to obtain a freedom that comes though service. Such service is ultimately grounded in trust in God, by whose loving grace we live and move and have our being.

God, whose service is perfect freedom, give us grace to put the needs and health of others before our own. Help us bear inconvenience for the sake of the greater release from sin and death you have given us in Jesus Christ our Lord. Amen

49 Handwashing

Pilate said to them, 'Then what should I do with Jesus who is called the Messiah?' All of them said, 'Let him be crucified!' Then he asked, 'Why, what evil has he done?' But they shouted all the more, 'Let him be crucified!'

So when Pilate saw that he could do nothing, but rather that a riot was beginning, he took some water and washed his hands before the crowd, saying, 'I am innocent of this man's blood; see to it yourselves.' Then the people as a whole answered, 'His blood be on us and on our children!' So he released Barabbas for them; and after flogging Jesus, he handed him over to be crucified.

MATTHEW 27:22–26

Before March 2020 most of us gave little thought to hand-sanitising gel. Those who work in hospitals and healthcare environments knew all about it, and the World Health Organization began to promote its use in 2009, especially in poor, less hygienic contexts. During the Covid-19 pandemic, sales of hand gel soared and at times it was hard to acquire. Whisky distilleries in Scotland converted their output, but the government began to tell us that using sanitising gel was not actually necessary; a thorough handwashing was equally effective.

There is some debate about whether hand sanitiser should be considered 'better' than ordinary handwashing. During the pandemic we were also reminded that soap and water can wash off a great deal of bacteria, dirt, grime and dust, and hand gel does not actually do that so well. On the other hand (as it were), some others say that bacteria are not killed by warm water and it is more ecologically harmful to heat the water and less effective. Another opinion is that

hand sanitisers are better against bacteria than warm soapy water, but less effective against viruses. Both techniques of handwashing require some basic training too: failing to wash all parts of the hands, such as between the fingers, undermines either approach. Nevertheless, whichever method is preferred, deploying it properly is a major weapon against infection from any disease.

It was only as recently as the 19th century that this was properly understood. One of the first people to recognise that sanitation in medical care is vital was Florence Nightingale (1820–1910). It was not simply her medical prowess as a pioneering nurse that enabled her to achieve such seminal influence, but also her mastery of statistics (which is less well-known). Having identified problems, she could represent them in a statistically convincing manner. She invented a form of pie chart, which is sometimes named after her. She also wrote theology: her outlook was founded in active care and love for others. She objected to religious discrimination, and is revered as a woman whose faith inspired world-changing thought and behaviour.

Equally significant but less celebrated is Ignaz Semmelweis (1818–65), a Hungarian pioneer of medical cleanliness. While working in the general hospital in Vienna in the 1840s, he observed a high rate of mortality among new mothers who contracted puerperal (childbed) fever, and he was the first to identify the gory fact that doctors were moving between morgues and maternity wards and so were infecting the women. A discipline of handwashing with chlorinated lime solution cut the death rate vastly.

Sadly no one believed Semmelweis, and fellow medics mocked him, preferring the time-honoured idea that infections were born in the air, being invariably foul-smelling. Semmelweis ended his days in an asylum where, beaten by the guards, he died from an infected wound. He was, however, right, and the later medical pioneers Louis Pasteur (1822–95) and Joseph Lister (1827–1912) made the lack of hand-hygiene precautions unthinkable. It is remarkable that this all happened so recently. In 1938 the Oscar for the best short film was awarded to *That Mothers Might Live*, a brief account of Semmelweis' world-changing work.

We have been washing our hands physically and metaphorically for thousands of years. Lady Macbeth notoriously could not wash off a spot of King Duncan's blood after inciting Macbeth to murder him, and ultimately it drives her to insanity and suicide. The connections with Pilate washing his hands of Jesus' execution cannot be overlooked, and we would want to say that neither Pilate nor Lady Macbeth, nor anyone else, can simply 'wash their hands' of something in order to exonerate themselves. We cannot walk away from sin or culpability just by rinsing our hands. The only water that can 'wash away sin' is baptismal water, metaphorically or sacramentally.

As mundane as handwashing is, it has always carried spiritual power and significance. Matthew's unique presentation of Pilate washing his hands is steeped in Jewish culture. None other than King David behaved in a similar way when it seemed he was going to be blamed for the death of Abner (2 Samuel 3:28–32). Meanwhile Deuteronomy 21:1–9 describes a ritual that Israelite elders were to do if someone was found dead outside their town, which involves them killing a heifer and washing their hands of its blood. This tradition, alongside Pilate's imitation of it, looks like strategic denial of something which is blatantly obvious. The elders kill the cow and Pilate sentences Jesus to death. Yet, hard as it is for many to appreciate then and ever since, saying that something is so and it being so are not the same thing, and the one does not bring about the other. Saying 'I am innocent' does not make me so, any more than saying 'I have washed my hands' makes them clean.

In Christianity handwashing is probably most associated with the actions of the priest at Holy Communion, where it may be customary to briefly and ritually rinse one's fingers in clean water, sometimes in a bowl called a lavabo. In some traditions the priest also prays from Psalm 26:6–7: 'I wash my hands in innocence, and go around your altar, O Lord, singing aloud a song of thanksgiving, and telling all your wondrous deeds.' While there may be an overtone of baptismal cleansing in this, the basic idea extends back to the sixth-century Rule of Benedict, who had his monks wash their hands before entering church. In a monastery there might be a large lavabo for this purpose, known as a *lavatorio*, from which we still derive a familiar word for a little room in which, among other things, handwashing takes place.

In our modern, virus-outwitting world, it is the ancient practice of handwashing that has carried us through, preserving and protecting so many of us. Next time you wash your hands, think of how Pilate's gesture means nothing in a world where sin can only be washed away by the living water of Christ.

Creator God, who gave us water to nourish and cleanse the earth, we thank you for the gift of hygiene with which to protect and heal. As water cleanses our bodies, heal us from the disease of sin by that living water of baptism, given to us as a constant reminder of the salvation poured out in the death and resurrection of Jesus Christ. Amen

Passiontide

50 Trees

'The trees once went out
    to anoint a king over themselves.
So they said to the olive tree,
    "Reign over us."
The olive tree answered them,
    "Shall I stop producing my rich oil
        by which gods and mortals are honoured,
        and go to sway over the trees?"
Then the trees said to the fig tree,
    "You come and reign over us."
But the fig tree answered them,
    "Shall I stop producing my sweetness
        and my delicious fruit,
        and go to sway over the trees?"
Then the trees said to the vine,
    "You come and reign over us."
But the vine said to them,
    "Shall I stop producing my wine
        that cheers gods and mortals,
        and go to sway over the trees?"
So all the trees said to the bramble,
    "You come and reign over us."

And the bramble said to the trees,
"If in good faith you are anointing me king over you,
then come and take refuge in my shade;
but if not, let fire come out of the bramble
and devour the cedars of Lebanon."'

JUDGES 9:8–15

There is a forest of trees in the Bible. From the tree of the knowledge of good and evil in the garden of Eden (Genesis 2:9) to the tree with the leaves for the healing of the nations in the New Jerusalem (Revelation 22:2), there are plenty to discover and shade beneath. There are broom trees, oaks, tamarind trees, cedars, fig trees, almond trees, mustard trees, sycamores, cypresses, firs, pomegranate trees, vines, olives and palms, apple trees, holm trees, plane trees and mulberry trees; leafy green trees and barren trees, withered trees and felled trees, good trees and bad trees. Many of these trees still exist in the Holy Land and most of them are so familiar to us that we barely notice them. Trees are vital for our survival on earth and have been around for 370 million years. And even though there are reputedly three trillion mature trees in the world, we take them for granted. Trees produce a variety of seeds and fruit for their own reproduction, some of which we have learned to harvest and enjoy, as the Old Testament parable of the trees demonstrates.

At this time of year there is one kind of tree which dominates our spirituality, and that is the tree of the cross. The cross is the true king of trees, on which the king of kings hung and died. Having grown up with the clean and polished symbol of Christianity, we can forget that Jesus was crucified not on a beautiful cross-shaped construction of smooth hewn planks, but a rough-cut trunk, against which a crosspiece was likely nailed. Although the Romans crucified Jesus, we cannot help be reminded – as the apostle Paul later was – of the Jewish law concerning such things: 'When someone is convicted of a crime punishable by death and is executed, and you hang him on a tree, his corpse must not remain all night upon the tree; you shall bury him that same day, for anyone hung on a tree is under God's curse' (Deuteronomy

21:22–23). Joshua had followed this rule too: 'And he hanged the king of Ai on a tree until evening; and at sunset Joshua commanded, and they took his body down from the tree' (Joshua 8:29).

One of the oldest poems in the English language, 'The Dream of the Rood', is a ninth-century meditation written from the perspective of the tree from which Christ's cross was hewn. At one with nature, the tree itself is wounded in the service of salvation:

> I remember the morning long ago
> when I was brought down at the edge of the forest
> severed from my roots.
> Strong enemies seized me,
> telling me to hold up their evil doers to the sky,
> and made of me a spectacle.
> Men bore me
> on their shoulders and set me on a hill.

The tree, personified, reflects upon its weighty task of bearing the Saviour of the world:

> Then the young warrior, God Almighty himself,
> stripped, and stood firm and without flinching.
> Bravely before the multitude he climbed upon the cross
> to save the world.
> I shivered when the hero clung to me.
> but I dared not bend to the ground,
> nor fall to the earth.
> I had to stand firm.
> I was a rood raised up.

The main medieval symbol of the cross found in a church was the rood – 'rood' or 'rod' was the name for cross, and it was found on the rood screen, which some churches still have, separating the chancel from the nave. In the Saxon poem, the 'scars of suffering' are on the branches of the holy rood, connecting the divine and the natural, heaven and earth, creature and creator. Our wounds, God's wounds and nature's wounds are inseparable.

> I bore on high the mighty King,
> the Lord of Heaven.
> I dared not stoop.
> They drove dark nails into me –
> see these terrible injuries,
> the open wounds of malice,
> I dared not injure the enemies.
> They insulted us both and I was soaked in the blood
> that ran from the Man's side after he set his spirit free.

The tree, a symbol of endurance and life, also suffers collateral damage in the conquest of sin:

> On that hill I saw and endured so much.
> I saw the God of Hosts stretched on the rack.
> I saw darkness covered the lifeless body of the ruler with clouds.
> Against his shining radiance
> Shadows swept across the land,
> strange powers moved under the clouds.
> All creation wept,
> weeping and moaning for the death of the King.
> For Christ was on the cross.

Trees are not only instruments of death or symbols of despair and defeat. For just as there is no cross without resurrection, and no eternal life without the cross, trees represent rejuvenation. Despairing Job reminds us of this:

> There is hope for a tree,
>   if it is cut down, that it will sprout again,
>   and that its shoots will not cease.
> Though its root grows old in the earth,
>   and its stump dies in the ground,

yet at the scent of water it will bud
and put forth branches like a young plant.

JOB 14:7–9

Any tree can remind us not only of Jesus' death, but also of his resurrection. These two events are the ground of Christian faith in which the church is rooted and to which all its branches testify. Ancient churchyards may have yew trees, which can be extremely long-lived, symbolising stability, eternal life and resurrection hope. Yet any tree can remind and inspire us with its trunk of faith, tender shoots of love and boughs of hope, reaching out to us in any of three trillion ways.

O Christ our King, who has rooted our faith in your death and resurrection for all people, and gives us the tree of life for the healing of the nations, we praise and adore you, for by your holy cross you have redeemed the world. Amen

51 Cinemas

Two bandits were crucified with him, one on his right and one on his left. Those who passed by derided him, shaking their heads and saying, 'You who would destroy the temple and build it in three days, save yourself! If you are the Son of God, come down from the cross.' In the same way the chief priests also, along with the scribes and elders, were mocking him, saying, 'He saved others; he cannot save himself. He is the King of Israel; let him come down from the cross now, and we will believe in him. He trusts in God; let God deliver him now, if he wants to; for he said, "I am God's Son."' The bandits who were crucified with him also taunted him in the same way.

From noon on, darkness came over the whole land until three in the afternoon. And about three o'clock Jesus cried with a loud voice, 'Eli, Eli, lema sabachthani?' that is, 'My God, my God, why have you forsaken me?' When some of the bystanders heard it, they said, 'This man is calling for Elijah.' At once one of them ran and got a sponge, filled it with sour wine, put it on a stick, and gave it to him to drink. But the others said, 'Wait, let us see whether Elijah will come to save him.' Then Jesus cried again with a loud voice and breathed his last… Now when the centurion and those with him, who were keeping watch over Jesus, saw the earthquake and what took place, they were terrified and said, 'Truly this man was God's Son!'

Many women were also there, looking on from a distance.

MATTHEW 27:38–50, 54–55A

During periods of lockdown, quarantine and isolation, television and films became something of a lifeline for many people, or at least a way to while away lonely hours. Meanwhile, cinema screens were silent for extended periods. Many missed that sense of occasion of going to the cinema, or indeed the theatre, ballet, opera or a concert. Some of the major venues took to streaming past recordings of productions, so one of the upsides of the early lockdowns was having the Royal Shakespeare Company or Royal Ballet broadcasting some of their major productions into our lounges, creating something of a theatrical event in our own homes. We could not go outside the front door much, but we could be transported into a London theatre and the imaginary world created by our greatest actors. The irony for them, of course, was that the theatres were closed and actors and musicians had a hard time of it for many months.

Films and other theatrical artforms are not just entertainment; there are layers of spiritual, sacred or religious meaning to be discovered. There are many biblical films, some of which are better and more authentic than others. Some inspire awe in themselves: *The Greatest Story Ever Told* is described on its cover as 'a magnificent film, handled with reverence, artistic appreciation and admirable restraint'. A true classic, released in 1965, we might put it alongside Franco Zeffirelli's 1977 *Jesus of Nazareth*, or Mel Gibson's brutally convincing *The Passion of the Christ* (2004). These and other interpretations of the ministry, life, death and resurrection of Jesus are often shown on television around Easter. They were shown in 2020 and 2021 when lockdowns prevented many going to church; we could at least watch one of these films on Good Friday: *The Greatest Story Ever Told* provides three hours and eleven minutes at the cross. There can be a discipline to selecting these films for Good Friday viewing and watching with reverential prayer, care and attention.

The 2016 film *Risen*, as its blurb puts it, 'is the epic biblical story of the resurrection, as told through the eyes of a non-believer. Clavius, a powerful military tribune, and his aide Lucius are tasked with solving the mystery of what happened to Jesus in the weeks following the crucifixion in order to disprove the rumours of a risen Messiah and prevent an uprising in Jerusalem.' These characters' names mean 'key' and 'light'. This inspirational but fictitious story is one for Easter Day perhaps.

The 2018 film *Mary Magdalene* is another creative enterprise with insight. One might be tempted by *Jesus Christ Superstar*, with its musical homages to just about every popular musical genre known in the 1970s, which is truly entertaining. Tim Rice's clever lyrics, following the success of *Joseph and the Amazing Technicolour Dreamcoat*, are a class act combined with Andrew Lloyd Webber's mastery of modern genres. But, viewer beware: these are interpretations, not retellings. The main thrust of Joseph is that 'any dream will do', and that you can succeed in anything if you try. *Jesus Christ Superstar* has no resurrection scene, makes Judas the central character and culminates in a multifaith singalong extolling the cult status of religious leaders as celebrities. It is fantastic in both senses of the word. 'Religious' movies and plays can be enjoyed, related to, but be careful about *believing* them.

Beyond retellings of biblical stories, other films deal with events or themes in church history. *Amazing Grace* is the story of the abolition of the slave trade, *Creation* is all about Charles Darwin and *Kingdom of Heaven* is all about the Crusades, while *Babette's Feast* is thoroughly eucharistic in its meaning. All of these are worth viewing through the lens of faith.

Any seriously good film can provoke spiritual reflection; one does not have to watch or read 'religious' content to be reflective or culturally mission-focused. All art is spiritual to some extent and bears scrutiny under the lens of the gospel. From *Pulp Fiction* to *Chocolat*, to the 'Matrix' series, there is always much to ponder. Many films (and the books they may be based on) have themes of redemption, forgiveness, salvation, grace, love – good and evil at their heart. I barely need mention Harry Potter, and other 'superheroes' are also worth pondering – Spiderman, Superman, Wonder Woman.

Modern culture has its favourite saviours of the world. Many action movies are not only about good conquering evil, but also about salvation; James Bond, for example, regularly saves the world. From the basic genre of fairy tales, in which everyone lives 'happily ever after', the superhero who comes to the rescue has evolved. It is not all damsels in distress now, thankfully, but whether it is overcoming the threat of an oversized gorilla, nuclear Armageddon or terrorist outrage, it invariably ends well.

As it does with Jesus Christ, the ultimate rescuer of humankind. Remember that next time you go to the cinema or watch a movie at home, for when Christ surveyed the world from a cross of shame, bearing the immense weight of sin and grief and pain, he was the superhero's superhero, not simply telling a great story, but bringing about a salvation that was, and still is, real and ever present.

God our Father, who sent your Son Jesus to be the Saviour of the world, keep us wakeful and watchful in your world, that we may see your glory all around. May all who are in danger or trouble today turn to him in their distress, that in sure and certain hope they may be rescued from grief and sin. Amen

Easter

52 Full circle: not the end

I consider that the sufferings of this present time are not worth comparing with the glory about to be revealed to us. For the creation waits with eager longing for the revealing of the children of God; for the creation was subjected to futility, not of its own will but by the will of the one who subjected it, in hope that the creation itself will be set free from its bondage to decay and will obtain the freedom of the glory of the children of God. We know that the whole creation has been groaning in labour pains until now; and not only the creation, but we ourselves, who have the first fruits of the Spirit, groan inwardly while we wait for adoption, the redemption of our bodies. For in hope we were saved. Now hope that is seen is not hope. For who hopes for what is seen? But if we hope for what we do not see, we wait for it with patience…

What then are we to say about these things? If God is for us, who is against us? He who did not withhold his own Son, but gave him up for all of us, will he not with him also give us everything else? Who will bring any charge against God's elect? It is God who justifies. Who is to condemn? It is Christ Jesus, who died, yes, who was raised, who is at the right hand of God, who indeed intercedes for us. Who will separate us from the love of Christ? Will hardship, or distress, or persecution, or famine, or nakedness, or peril, or sword? As it is written, 'For your sake we are being killed all day long; we are accounted as sheep to be slaughtered.'

No, in all these things we are more than conquerors through him who loved us. For I am convinced that neither death, nor life, nor angels, nor rulers, nor things present, nor things to come, nor powers, nor height, nor depth, nor anything else in all creation, will be able to separate us from the love of God in Christ Jesus our Lord.

ROMANS 8:18–25, 31–39

You might remember my seven Rs of Lent (see page 191): regret, repentance, recognition, resolution, reconciliation, renewal and resurrection. These seven take us on a journey from our own fallen nature to the cross and beyond. They bear us onward in faith, hope and love. The dark journey of Lent can carry us to the heart of our souls, there to examine ourselves, to regret, repent and recognise our human frailty, but then to resolve to be reconciled and renewed by the saving grace of God brought to and bought for us by our Lord Jesus Christ, who died, was buried and rose again, to bring us resurrection life.

The seventh Sunday of Lent is, of course, Easter Day, which is not part of Lent. Lent is over. We have journeyed and reflected, and what we have laid down in Lent we can pick up, if we wish. What we have taken up, we can put down, if we wish. Or perhaps we have been changed by the privations or the resolutions, the new routines. We may find that the thing we gave up, we are better off without; or that what we decided to start doing, we have found enjoyable, useful or worthy. There is no rule that says we have to resume what we gave up or stop what we started. We have crossed the finishing line of Lent, but we can carry on going if we can or wish. In any event, perhaps we have found the grace of God leading us and helping us, and we therefore have emerged from Lent a different person in a different world. This is true even if we 'failed' to maintain our Lenten fast: we have still learned about ourselves, and about God.

For it has been quite a journey, has it not? We have arrived at the end, both of Lent and of this book. You may even have spent a year reading it. We have been 'out and about' in what we might call a post-Covid world, although always acknowledging that Covid-19 has not gone away; it remains part of our lives and it could rear an ugly head again, even repeat its paralysis of the world as it did in 2020. Hopefully, there have been many lessons learned alongside the suffering and the saving, the treatments and the vaccines, the politics and the policies.

For those of us in the UK, the pandemic succeeded Brexit seamlessly: the virus landed on our shores just as we redefined our borders. Two years later, the British government declared all restrictions lifted, in England at least, and within hours Vladimir Putin's war machine crossed into neighbouring Ukraine, causing the greatest refugee migration in post-war history and bringing something new and horrible to stretch our compassion, kindness and resilience. Many have had to bear the brunt of bombs and bullets, and their suffering continues. If we look back over the past few years, they have likely not been the happiest years, and with hindsight many people were perhaps living in a relatively carefree context before 2020. We can lament in a spirit of Lent, and it is good and right to do so, during Lent. The focus on mortality, repentance and self-denial that Lent offers us is fitting as we look back on the past few years.

Yet it is now Easter, and it is time to look forward in the light of another, new dawn. We cannot, and should not, live in Lent always. For we are Easter people, and 'Alleluia' is our song. Every day is Easter Day, in fact. Whatever happens, things present, things to come, powers, heights, depths, anything in all creation, nothing can separate us from the love of God in Christ Jesus our Lord. Paul's words of hope and faith to the church in Rome resonate especially well in our recent times, when daily death tallies were almost a ritual on news programmes for many months. Yet God is for us, not against us, through thick walls of lockdown and thinly veiled fear. The sufferings of our recent times are part of a bigger picture, of suffering, yes – there will always be suffering, it seems – but also of redemption and hope. We have waited – and continue to wait – in patient hope. It is the Easter dawn, the newly kindled fire of light and promise that illuminates our faith with the assurance of love, all of which comes to us through faith in Jesus Christ.

With Lent over, we now celebrate with joy the magnificent day on which our Lord Jesus Christ, crucified on Good Friday, rose from the dead and appeared to first a few and then many disciples. Improbable and impossible, unbelievable but believed by billions of people today, we join with the worldwide community of faith in proclaiming 'Alleluia – Christ is risen. He is risen indeed, Alleluia!'

Our God of love and mercy, hear our prayers as we reflect on the passing of time and the events of recent years. As we are borne onwards by tides of uncertainty, give us grace to look back with love, and to journey in Easter faith and live in eternal hope, revealed in the glorious dawn of resurrection hope and joy. Amen

Questions for reflection and discussion

It is good to talk. The past few years have been difficult for many, and unique for most of us, whatever age we are. The pandemic period has been compared to other periods in history, which we may or may not have lived through, but in any event it has been a common experience, although experienced differently by each one of us. In this way, it is not unlike the reading of scripture. You will have read this book by yourself, in your own context. Parts of it will have inspired, influenced, even annoyed you more than others. You might have laughed, cried or shouted at the pages.

Discussion and reflection are an opportunity that can come as a good consequence of reading the same thing that others are reading simultaneously. Separated by space, as each reads alone, we are yet connected by the common food of scripture, taken in our own time at our own pace. We each chew on it in our own way, drawing different flavours, sensations and preferences, although the food does not change; spinach is spinach, however you serve it!

Yet discussion or shared reflection on these chapters might aid digestion, so here are some open questions to enable conversation in a Bible study or other group who gather to take further what is published here. The questions may also aid personal devotion. Use them as you wish and may God bless and inspire you on your journey as you read, mark and inwardly digest the scripture, reason and tradition that informs this book.

Remember there are no right or wrong answers – these questions are simply to enable a group to engage in conversation. Discuss the whole book, or any number of a collection of chapters.

- What do you think is the main idea or purpose of this book? Did that come across strongly?

- Have any of the topics discussed touched on personal – or shared – aspects of your life?

- Have any specific chapters struck or touched you personally? If so, how and why, do you think? Is God speaking to you through scripture and reflection?

- For any given chapter: what does the object or activity under discussion have to teach us about your life, faith or relationships?

- Are there any other passages of scripture, or objects that can speak to us about the past few years? What might have been included in this book that has not been?

- When you look back at the pandemic years of 2020–21 and reflect upon them, what emotions do you feel? What, under God, have we learned, as individuals, communities and society?

- What does the pandemic look like viewed through the ensuing lenses of the invasion of Ukraine, recent political worries, energy and cost-of-living crises and the death of Her Majesty The Queen?

- Was anything completely new to you? Any 'eureka' or jaw-dropping moments? If so, what difference will that make?

- Which do you prefer: scripture informing daily modern life, or modern life shining a new light on scripture?

- Have you read *At Home in Advent* and/or *At Home in Lent*? Is this a worthy successor?

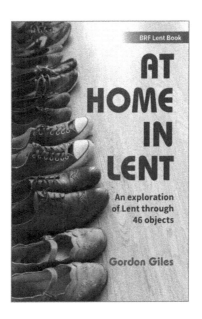

Here is an original way of approaching Lent, one that will encourage you to consider your own faith journey in the light of the Easter story. Inspired by Neil MacGregor's Radio 4 programme *A History of the World in 100 Objects*, Gordon Giles spends each week in a different room gleaning spiritual lessons from everyday household objects. As a result, you might discover that finding God in the normal pattern of life – even in the mundane – transforms how you approach each day.

At Home in Lent
An exploration of Lent through 46 objects
Gordon Giles
978 0 85746 589 4 £8.99

brfonline.org.uk

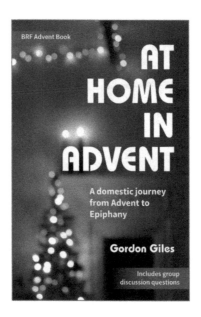

Following on from the success of *At Home in Lent*, Gordon Giles takes a journey through Advent to Christmas and beyond in the company of familiar seasonal and domestic objects and experiences. Focusing on the everyday stuff we typically associate with this time of year, including some things not so festive, he reflects on their spiritual significance, meaning and message in today's world. Beginning with chapters on journeying and travel, the book moves though major Advent themes of expectation, waiting, mortality and hope to the joy of incarnation and salvation.

At Home in Advent
A domestic journey from Advent to Epiphany
Gordon Giles
978 0 85746 980 9 £8.99

brfonline.org.uk

Sustaining your daily journey with the Bible

New Daylight is ideal for anyone wanting an accessible yet stimulating aid to spending time with God each day, deepening their faith and their knowledge of scripture. Each issue provides four months of daily Bible readings and comment, with a team of regular contributors drawn from a range of church backgrounds and covering a varied selection of Old and New Testament, biblical themes, characters and seasonal readings. Each daily section includes a short Bible passage (text included), thought-provoking comment and a prayer or point for reflection.

New Daylight is edited by Gordon Giles and is published three times a year in January, May and September. Available in regular and deluxe editions with large print, as a daily email and as an app for Android, iPhone and iPad.

brfonline.org.uk

Enabling all ages to grow in faith

Anna Chaplaincy
Living Faith
Messy Church
Parenting for Faith

BRF is a Christian charity that resources individuals and churches. Our vision is to enable people of all ages to grow in faith and understanding of the Bible and to see more people equipped to exercise their gifts in leadership and ministry.

To find out more about our work, visit
brf.org.uk